# 500

## Are We at the Dawn of a New Era of Glory?

Jarrod Cooper

RIVER
PUBLISHING

River Publishing & Media Ltd
Bradbourne Stables
East Malling
Kent ME19 6DZ
United Kingdom

info@river-publishing.co.uk

ISBN 978-1-908393-74-6
Cover design by www.spiffingcovers.com
Printed in the United Kingdom

# Contents

# Introduction

In July 2017, I sat outside The Queen's House, Greenwich, looking up towards the Royal Observatory, home of the Prime Meridian of the World – the site from where we get Greenwich Mean Time (GMT). It is the place where east meets west; the place from which we on earth interpret solar time and align our clocks. This dates back to 1884 when the Greenwich Meridian was recommended as the Prime Meridian of the world at the International Meridian Conference. It means that the Prime Meridian at Greenwich is the centre of world time and the basis for our global system of time zones.

You could say it is a picture of where the movement of the heavens are interpreted to give us timings on the earth.

Here I was, on a summer prayer and study sabbatical, looking out from an ancient royal home, towards the spot where we look to the heavens to discern our times.

So, of course, God spoke to me!

I had been living with a word from God for about 8 months – a word about the significance of the 2017, 500-year anniversary of the commencement of the Reformation – when Martin Luther sent lasting ripples of transformation through the world, simply by questioning the status quo. In

October 1517, 500 years ago, Luther had begun a powerful and surprising work of restoration in the Church. This led me to ask if a 500-year era might have been significant in history before...

The Bible reveals that God has often moved in specific seasons. Daniel 2:21 states that God,

*"Changes times and seasons; He deposes kings and raises up others..."*

And that He,

*"...gives wisdom to the wise and knowledge to the discerning."*

Acts 17:26 says that God, *"determines our pre-appointed times."* We also read in 1 Chronicles 12:32 that the sons of Issachar, *"...had understanding of the times to know what Israel ought to do."*

God loves to reveal His seasons and timings to His people. So, is the 500-year marker in 2017 an important season-change for us today?

As I sat looking at the place where man explores the heavens and interprets the timings of the earth, God began to speak. This is what I heard...

# Chapter One
# The 500-Year Era

Numbers are incredibly important in the Bible.

## The Number 3

Jesus was raised on the third day. The three righteous patriarchs before the flood were Abel, Enoch and Noah. After the flood there were the righteous "fathers", Abraham, Isaac and Jacob. Jesus prayed three times in the Garden of Gethsemane before His arrest. He was placed on the cross at the third hour of the day and died at the ninth hour. Three is the number of resurrection.

## The Number 7

The number seven defines a week, appearing immediately in Genesis 1 as God creates the world in six days and rests on the seventh. Thus it represents perfection and completion. I often find that my life is defined by seven-year cycles. Every seven years I seem to adjust in my role, my positioning, and the outworking of my purpose. If I'm honest, when I'm being a bit dull, it sometimes takes eight or nine years (I can be slow to hear!). But when I'm on the ball, I know something is shifting after six years and I'm ready! Anyone else sense that?

## The Number 12

There were twelve tribes and twelve disciples. God required that twelve unleavened cakes of bread were placed each week before His presence. Christ's bride (the Church) in Revelation wears a crown with twelve stars. The New Jerusalem has twelve gates made of pearl. Over each gate will be one of the names of Israel's twelve tribes. The number twelve is often thought to represent God's power and authority.

## The Number 40

Forty is a powerful number of transition in the Bible. It rained for forty days in Noah's time, as the wicked world was washed away. Moses spent forty days on the mountain of God as the Law was revealed. Spies explored the land for forty days as they prepared to enter in, but they failed and endured forty years in the desert! Elijah journeyed forty days to the mountain of God to transition into a new season. Jesus spent forty days in the wilderness as He moved into His ministry, and then appeared to His disciples for forty days as He prepared for the new Church age. God does a lot of stuff in 40's!

## The Number 500

Did you know that the number 500 is important too? Most importantly, the number 500 might well deeply affect your life today if you live within a few decades of 2017.

Throughout known biblical and Church history, approximately every 500 years it would appear that some radical change takes place that affects how God interacts with mankind, or how we understand and grasp God's divine purpose.

By this I do not mean that everything changes at exactly 500 years to the minute, as the clock strikes midnight! I mean, rather, that God moves, like the slow turn of a giant battleship changing course in the ocean, about every 500 years or so. Every five centuries God's purposes on earth seem to haul us into a new age, slowly carving a new course on the seas of history, the change sometimes taking several decades to emerge. Like a heavy castle gate, swinging slowly on giant hinges, God takes mankind through a colossal historical adjustment that ultimately leads to the unfolding of His purpose for humanity.

> **And you are alive at one of those turning points in history!**

Let me take you back in history through eight 500-year eras, so you can see that something extraordinary has taken place at each pivotal time.

## Abraham and His Family

A little over 4000 years ago, God began to interact with a man called Abram (whose name He later changed to Abraham). It was Abraham who first understood the Gospel (Galatians 3:8). He was the father of faith. Today we are called the children of Abraham (Romans 4:16), because we, like Abraham, receive our righteousness through trusting God; faith, not works. This was a significant announcement of God's heart for friendship with man on planet earth. God used the powerful pictures of giving Abraham a family (his wife was barren) and promising them a land of their own (they were nomadic). You only have to watch the news today to see how this historic, pivotal period in time has affected the world. Slowly, through miracle after miracle, God revealed His purposes for Abraham's line: three generations of barren women had miraculous births, their children eventually becoming what we call today the Children of Israel.

About 500 years after Abraham came Moses…

## Moses

Moses was another remarkable and pivotal "friend of God". He was the one sent to set God's people free following 400 years of slavery. He brought them God's Law and helped them to enter Abraham's Promised Land. He spoke face to face with God. At times his face shone with God's glory. He is one of the greatest figures in our biblical history.

About 500 years after Moses came David…

## David

David was the young *"man after God's own heart"* (Acts 13:22; 1 Samuel 13:14). He was the worshipper in the field who made Israel a worshipping nation. He was the first to remove the veil between the Holy Place and the Most Holy Place, signalling that an unveiling of God's powerful glory would one day come to the earth. Even though David failed morally, Jesus was still called the "Son of David", after this major figure. In the last days, the book of Acts tells us that God will rebuild the Tabernacle of David, so significant was this biblical hero (Acts 15:16).

About 500 years after David the nation was in turmoil…

## Exile and Turmoil

About 500 years after King David's reign, the Children of Israel were in exile. Jerusalem had been ransacked, the temple destroyed and then later rebuilt, leading to 400 years of biblical "silence", during which time it seemed that God did not speak to the Jews. They were waiting for a Messiah who came, of course, in the form of Jesus.

About 500 years after the exile came Jesus and the early Church…

## Jesus

Jesus is the most obvious of all great pivotal points in our history. When He came, He split history in two, B.C. and A.D. He is also the pivot between Old Testament and New; between Law and Grace; between flesh and the empowerment of the Spirit!

> **Jesus, the cross and His resurrection**
> **IS the pivotal point of all history.**

It is amazing that Jesus came just after the birth of the Roman empire in 31BC, allowing the Gospel to spread rapidly along those straight Roman roads. But in AD476, about 500 years after Jesus' time on earth, the Roman empire declined and we entered the Dark Ages.

## The Dark Ages

As the Roman empire declined, the Dark Ages began, heralding a demographic, cultural and economic deterioration. During this time the Church continued to spread beyond the old Roman reaches, but lacked the widespread power of the Holy

Spirit, miracles, signs and wonders that had marked its early years. Church had become a bastion of humanised political power, financial gain and corruption, where people paid to have their sins "forgiven" and to lessen their time in purgatory. Though not completely devoid of all virtue, this was largely a "night time" for the Church's true purpose. It lost the innocent passion that had been so evident in its genesis.

500 years after the Dark Ages began, we find the Great Schism...

## The Great Schism

In 1054 AD the Great Schism occurred – the break in the communion between what are now the Eastern Orthodox and Roman Catholic churches. The schism was caused by endless arguments, infighting and the politicising of power and authority across the Church. The Great Schism was essentially the forerunner of the Protestant Reformation, with a refusal to accept the unbiblical concept of the supremacy of Rome at its core.

## 500 Years Ago

After the Great Schism, 500 years ago, came the Reformation...

## The Reformation

After 1000 years of comparative Church powerlessness, a man called Martin Luther was about to become another pivotal character in global history. On All Saints' Eve, 1517AD, when Luther publicly objected to the way preacher Johann Tetzel was selling "indulgences" (the aforementioned way of reducing the amount of punishment one had to undergo for sins) he famously nailed his 95 Theses to a castle church door, calling for a public debate. His Theses spread across Germany, causing shockwaves as he questioned the authority of the Pope, a move which ultimately led to a transformation we can still feel the effects of today.

Luther was a man of faith who stood against the corrupt political power games that characterised the Church. He stood for the authority of Scripture and the doctrine of salvation by grace.

> *Little did he know that his actions would usher in 500 years of Reformation that would ultimately bring the Church back to her original passion, power and purpose.*

Across the last 500 years, wave after wave of reforming and restoring power has washed the Church, bringing her back to God's original design.

One writer stated,

"Luther's legacy is immense and cannot be adequately summarised. Every Protestant Reformer – like Calvin, Zwingli, Knox, and Cranmer – and every Protestant stream –Lutheran, Reformed, Anglican and Anabaptist – were inspired by Luther in one way or another. On a larger canvas, his reform unleashed forces that ended the Middle Ages and ushered in the modern era."

> *Martin Luther has been called, "the last medieval man and the first modern one."*

Following in the wake of Luther's legacy came many wave-riders of Reformation, including the likes of John Calvin, John Knox and George Fox. By the 1700s, men like Jonathan Edwards,

George Whitefield, William Wilberforce and John and Charles Wesley had emerged. John Wesley preached with power and men fell, thunderstruck by God's presence and conviction. He and his contemporaries turned Great Britain upside down as they added personal holiness and sanctification of conduct to Luther's concept of personal, intimate faith. These reforming revivals continued their transformative work through men like Charles Finney, Spurgeon, DL Moody, and countless others who called the Church back to its radical, original roots.

While Luther restored the concept of salvation by grace, and Wesley that faith should lead to a changed lifestyle, by 1880 onwards the Latter Rain movement and the Pentecostals burst onto the scene with a reformed sense of God's power. The Holy Spirit began to move in ways that had not been seen since the days of the early Church, especially with widespread speaking in tongues. The concept of tongues had, for many centuries, been something worthy only of historic note, and that on rare occasions. Today, a little over 100 years since the gift seemed to resurge across the planet, millions speak in tongues every day.

At the early dawn of the 1900s, the Welsh Revival and the Azusa Street Revival in the U.S., along with several other areas of remarkable outpouring, caused a new surge. A tangible sense of God's presence, words of knowledge, healing and miracles were restored to the Church (and not without controversy!)

Following the Pentecostal outpouring came decades of healing revivals. Truly remarkable miracles, signs and wonders led to thousands upon thousands of lives being transformed under the ministries of William Branham, Oral Roberts and many other lesser-known ministries like A. A. Allen and Jack Coe. This led to the Church being reformed in the area of the miraculous. Today, more people are healed through miraculous prayer than ever before in history.

Hot on the heels of the healing revivals came a restoration of faith, deliverance, prosperity, intercession, Spirit-filled worship, and new understandings of the end times and our sonship in Christ. While some have taken these restored truths to unhealthy extremes, in the main they have been beautifully and powerfully restored to much of the Body of Christ.

## God Has Been Rebuilding the Church

Looking back, it appears as though God has been remodelling the Church, brick by brick:

- Faith for salvation
- Sanctification of lifestyle
- Outpouring of the Spirit
- Speaking in tongues
- Healings
- Miracles
- Prosperity
- Deliverance
- Intercession
- Spirit-filled worship

Wave after wave of truth, bringing wave after wave of restored strength. God has been rebuilding His temple, the Church, for 500 years.

In my own living memory I can recount two final stages that emerged during the 1980s and 1990s. These two fascinate me, as they speak into the very structure of the house of God, His temple in the world:

## Prophets Restored

When I was young, it would have been considered incredibly

arrogant to call yourself a Prophet. For some reason, everyone was happy with Pastors and Teachers, and we let the Evangelists travel (because they were too crazy for the local church!) But the role of Prophet had been lost. There were a few, but these were only ever considered remarkably gifted and "rare" men and women who could hear God with unnerving accuracy, understand the times and bring a powerful sense that God was very present in His awesome power.

But in the 1980s (the timing is based on my personal recollection) prophets began to burst onto the scene as never before. And not just a rare few, but prophets who were training up "Companies of Prophets" and starting "Schools of Prophecy". Thus, suddenly, men and women who could prophesy accurately and powerfully began to number in the hundreds, then thousands. Today, many thousands operate as prophets and declare God's word. The role of Prophet has been reformed and restored to the Church across the world.

## Apostles Restored

Similarly, as a young lad in the 1970s I was aware that very few would have called themselves "Apostle" without being considered arrogant. But in the 1990s the role of Apostle as architect, strategist, overseer and "chief coach" to the Church began to arise. At first, it was just a few key figures, but today thousands of apostles and apostolic networks are releasing church planting, missions strategies, church health and signs and wonders across the world!

## The Five-Fold Ministry Restored

And so, in addition to many other truths restored, the Church is now beginning to learn to operate with a healthy and full, five-fold leadership in place. Truly She is beginning to look like a temple that may just be ready to do something extraordinary in the earth, by God's grace.

Ephesians 4:11-13 states of these five vital ministries that we call, "The Five-fold",

> *"Christ Himself gave the apostles, the prophets, the evangelists, the pastors and teachers, to equip His people for works of service, so that the body of Christ may be built up until we all reach unity in the faith and in the knowledge of the Son of God and become mature, attaining to the whole measure of the fullness of Christ."*

The restoration of Apostles and Prophets speaks of completion – the Apostle being the final piece to be restored. It is the final piece because it is the highest form of Christ's servant authority on the earth. The apostle Paul clearly designated their position when he noted, *"God has placed in the Church, **first apostles**, second prophets..."* (1 Corinthians 12:28).

> The current apostolic surge across the earth, coupled with the fact that God moves and adjusts His activity on the earth every 500 years, means that the Reformation might well be over, and something new is about to begin.

We are at the end, or you could say the beginning, of a new era today. This is not just the turning of a page, or a new chapter, but the start of a new Church Age.

And YOU are alive for such a time as this!

I am so glad I wasn't born 1000 years ago, when the Church was politicised, powerless and largely devoid of miracles.

The Bible wasn't even available in English, or other everyday languages, so biblical knowledge was reserved for an elite few. I'm glad I wasn't born when we didn't understand grace, faith, personal intimacy with God, the availability of prophecy or the joy of Spirit filled worship!

> You and I have been born in a privileged time – when God is moving as never before in the earth.

More people are being raised from the dead than ever before in Church history. I even know of churches that have "Resurrection teams". There are ministries that have seen a few raised from the dead, but others that have seen hundreds! HUNDREDS!

More people are Spirit filled than ever in history.

More Muslims are having visions of Jesus and are coming to the Messiah than ever in history!

More people are being born again than ever in history!

If you were to stand back and look at the world from the balcony of heaven, you would see that these are extraordinary days. On the Day of Pentecost, 3,000 were saved. During the Welsh Revival, one hundred years ago, a few hundred thousand were saved. Yet, I have been in a single service where over 1 million have received Christ in one evening! These are remarkable days!

But the great question now is, what comes next? We are not only at the END of an era, we are at the BEGINNING of a new era. What will that era look like? What is going to happen next? Has God's Reformation work finished? How will Church change in the next 500 years, should Jesus tarry?

## The Picture of a Jewish Day

Finally, as a little picture of what God might be up to, I want you to consider the Jewish day. A Jewish day starts in the evening (not in the morning, as we Westerners think). That is why it says in Genesis, at creation, *"...and there was the evening, and the morning – the first day"* (Genesis 1:5).

So the Jewish day starts in the evening and is followed by the night, and then comes the morning and the fullness of day. I believe this is a picture of how the Church age is unfolding since Jesus' time on earth.

Jesus and the early Church (which we often think must have been the pinnacle), was actually just the evening. That is why Jesus says we will do greater things than He ever did (John 14:12). If Jesus and the early Church was the evening, then the fall of the Roman Empire, ushering in the Dark Ages, brought 1000 years of relative "night time" for the Church.

But 500 years ago dawn broke through with the morning star of the Reformation. Since that time, wave after wave of fresh, divine sunlight has bathed us in God's purposes. As the Proverb says,

> *"The path of the righteous is as the first gleam of dawn, growing ever brighter to the full light of day"* (Proverbs 4:18).

I believe we are the generation of the full light of day! We are to surpass what Jesus and the early Church saw (not because of our own virtue, but because of His purpose!) and we will see the last days of God's purpose on earth – the great culmination of His redemption and salvation.

The evening and the night are behind us. We are marching into the full brightness of God's purposes on the earth. You were not born for the dark ages, but for the great, bright hope of the purposes of God! He has truly saved the best wine until last (John 2:10).

Aren't you so glad you are alive today?!

# Chapter Two
# An Age of Glory

But what exactly is God up to? If the season of reformation and restoration is over, what does that mean?

The picture of God building a family, tabernacle or temple, and then covering it, or filling it with glory, is one common to Scripture. I think these verses may give us a clue as to the purposes of God in the earth in this next age, now that the Church is restored:

*"When all the work Solomon had done for the temple of the LORD was finished, he brought in the things his father David had dedicated—the silver and gold and all the furnishings—and he placed them in the treasuries of God's temple. Then Solomon summoned to Jerusalem the elders of Israel, all the heads of the tribes and the chiefs of the Israelite families, to bring up the ark of the LORD's covenant from Zion, the City of David. When all the elders of Israel had arrived, the Levites took up the ark, and they brought up the ark and the tent of meeting and all the sacred furnishings in it.*

*The priests then brought the ark of the LORD's covenant*

*to its place in the inner sanctuary of the temple, the Most Holy Place, and put it beneath the wings of the cherubim. The cherubim spread their wings over the place of the ark and covered the ark and its carrying poles.*

*The priests then withdrew from the Holy Place. All the Levites who were musicians—Asaph, Heman, Jeduthun and their sons and relatives—stood on the east side of the altar, dressed in fine linen and playing cymbals, harps and lyres. They were accompanied by 120 priests sounding trumpets. The trumpeters and musicians joined in unison to give praise and thanks to the LORD. Accompanied by trumpets, cymbals and other instruments, the singers raised their voices in praise to the LORD and sang:*

*'He is good; His love endures forever.'*

*Then the temple of the LORD was filled with the cloud, and the priests could not perform their service because of the cloud, for the glory of the LORD filled the temple of God."* (2 Chronicles 5:1-14)

Once Solomon had built the temple in a way that pleased God, God came in glory. Solomon built the temple, restored the Ark and other furnishings to their rightful places, then God came in His splendour, so powerfully that, *"The priests could not perform their duties"* (v14). It's like God was so pleased that He took over!

The lesson here is that a completed (you might say, restored) temple is ready for the glory of God to inhabit it.

> **Could it be that a restored Church is also ready for the glory and splendour of God to inhabit like never before?**

## An Age of Glory

*"For the earth will be filled with the knowledge of the glory of the LORD as the waters cover the sea."* (Habakkuk 2:14)

I believe that is what is about to follow the last 500 years of Reformation, is an age of *Glory*. God has finished building, restoring, reforming. He has put faith at the heart of our relationship with Him again. He has shown how this must be outworked in the way we conduct our lives. He has poured out the power of His Spirit, with speaking in tongues. He has stirred us to expect miracles, healings, remarkable signs and wonders. He has been delivering us from a *poverty spirit* and envisioning us for a remarkable end-times harvest.

Finally, in the last few decades He has restored the two vital, foundational, structural elements the Church needs to be mature and complete: the restoration of the apostles and the prophets. These are of huge importance:

*"Consequently, you are no longer foreigners and strangers, but fellow citizens with God's people and also members of His household, built on the foundation of the apostles and prophets, with Christ Jesus Himself as the chief cornerstone. In Him the whole building is joined together and rises to become a holy temple in the Lord. And in Him you too are being built together to become a dwelling in which God lives by His Spirit."* (Ephesians 2:19-22)

Apostles and prophets are foundational to working with Christ to become a healthy, fully-functioning Church. Apostles bring a sense of divine strategy and alignment to God's masterplan.

Prophets bring the sense of the imminent power and voice of God, never allowing us to be content with theory or principle alone.

On their own, pastors and teachers might be overly concerned with the happiness of the flock, or great theoretical teaching, but when they team up with apostles and prophets, the Church comes alive with power, pioneering ventures and divine unction. When the evangelists join the picture, with all their passion to reach the world, we begin to see a fully functioning "temple", ready for the glory to be poured out!

This time, let's read these verses in full:

*"But to each one of us grace has been given as Christ apportioned it. This is why it says:*
*'When He ascended on high,*
*he took many captives*
*and gave gifts to His people.'*

*(What does 'He ascended' mean except that He also descended to the lower, earthly regions? He who descended is the very one who ascended higher than all the heavens, in order to fill the whole universe). So Christ Himself gave the apostles, the prophets, the evangelists, the pastors and teachers, to equip His people for works of service, so that the body of Christ may be built up until we all reach unity in the faith and in the knowledge of the Son of God and become mature, attaining to the whole measure of the fullness of Christ.*

*Then we will no longer be infants, tossed back and forth by the waves, and blown here and there by every wind of teaching and by the cunning and craftiness of people in their deceitful scheming. Instead, speaking the truth in love, we will grow to become in every respect the mature body of him who is the*

24

*head, that is, Christ. From him the whole body, joined and held together by every supporting ligament, grows and builds itself up in love, as each part does its work."* (Ephesians 4:7-16)

Here Ephesians shows us that the five-fold ministers don't exist to do all the work of the Church. Rather, they equip and mature the entire body, *"until we all reach unity in the faith and in the knowledge of the Son of God and become mature, attaining to the whole measure of the fullness of Christ."* (v13)

Oh, I love that verse! It means that, fully restored, we will step up into the FULLNESS of CHRIST, when the five-fold ministries are operating properly.

And in the last few decades they have indeed been finding their place, learning to walk in their true identity with humility, losing all the false nonsense regarding abuses of power and becoming true foot-washing, authoritative fathers in the faith and servants of the Church.

This means we are ready for a new Church era that you might call "The Full Measure of Christ" or "The Church in Full Maturity". Perhaps we would call it "The Glorious Bride" or "Christ in Us, the Hope of Glory". Call it what you want, I believe those with the eyes of the Spirit can see God at work, bringing us into a new Church age.

> **Whichever way we say it, when the temple is built, the GLORY is poured into it!**

God comes – not to visit, but to inhabit. To dwell. To be the sap in the Vine called Christ, so that fruit bursts forth from our branches, bringing glory to Him as we work in union with His Spirit!

25

As Ephesians 2:22 puts it, *"...in him you too are being built together to become a dwelling in which God lives by his Spirit."* This is the purpose of heaven.

## Defining Glory

In the Bible, the "glory" of God is described in several ways. It can simply mean the praise of God. But the glory that filled the temple was so much more than simply praise and exaltation. This was a visible presence; an evident manifestation of the might of God.

In Hebrew, the word used for the glory that filled the temple was דּוֹבָכ (*kabowd*), which speaks of "abundance" and "splendour". A cloud of abundant splendour became visible as the pleasure of God "moved in" to the temple.

The root of the word *kabowd* literally means the weightiness, or heaviness, of God. This was no light presence, this was the heavy-weight fulness of God; a sign and a wonder that God's might was present.

This same glory appeared to the Children of Israel in Moses' time. In Exodus 24:17 we read,

*"And the sight of the glory of the LORD was like devouring fire on the top of the mount in the eyes of the children of Israel."*

It is the same glory that passed by Moses, when God placed him in the cleft of the rock. In Exodus 40:34-35 it says,

*"Then a cloud covered the tent of the congregation, and the glory of the LORD filled the tabernacle. And Moses was not able to enter into the tent of the congregation, because the*

cloud abode thereon, and the glory of the LORD filled the tabernacle."

Deuteronomy 5:24 says,

"The LORD our God has shown us His glory and His majesty, and we have heard His voice from the fire."

God's glory came as visible fire, as cloud. When He moved in provision, He showed His glory.

> God's glory is something that appears, is revealed and can be seen.

God's glory can be manifest in a thunderstorm (according to Job), and it is seen in plagues and other miracles; in the cloudy pillar; in the theophany at Mount Sinai; in the fire initiating the sacrificial system and in the Ark of the Covenant.

2 Chronicles 7 goes on to say,

"Now when Solomon had made an end of praying, the fire came down from heaven, and consumed the burnt offering and the sacrifices; and the glory of the LORD filled the house. And the priests could not enter into the house of the LORD, because the glory of the LORD had filled the LORD's house."

Haggai 2:7 says of God's glory, "And I will shake all nations, and the desire of all nations shall come: and I will fill this house with glory, says the LORD of hosts", while 2:9 promises, "'The glory of this latter house shall be greater than of the former,' says the LORD of hosts: 'and in this place will I give peace.'"

In the New Testament the word for this manifest glory

is δόξα (*doxa*), meaning "judgement, opinion, splendour, brightness, magnificence, excellence, pre-eminence, dignity, grace and majesty" – God in His most glorious state. It is what the disciples, Peter, James and John, saw on the Mount of Transfiguration (Luke 9).

## Show Me Your Glory

*"Then Moses said, 'Now show me your glory.' And the LORD said, 'I will cause all my goodness to pass in front of you, and I will proclaim my name, the LORD, in your presence. I will have mercy on whom I will have mercy, and I will have compassion on whom I will have compassion. But,' he said, 'you cannot see my face, for no one may see me and live.'"* (Exodus 33:18-20)

In this passage Moses is encountering God and asks of Him, "Show me your glory." The response of the Father is interesting, as He simply says, "I will cause all my goodness to pass in front of you."

Here we find a beautiful definition for the glory of God:

> **It is God's goodness made manifest.**

So often God is working in hidden places, manoeuvring, adjusting, protecting. My friend Gerald Coates likes to say, "He's doing more behind our backs than in front of our faces." So true! But when He leaps from the background and reveals His power and splendour for all to see – that's the glory of God! God, visible.

When Jesus turned water into wine we read that, *"He thus revealed His glory"* (John 2:11). When He healed people, walked on water, when He provided, protected, announced Himself or revealed Himself – these are the glory of God at work.

## Greater Glory

In the Old Testament we seem to see much of the glory of God at work, especially in the life of Moses, as we've already read. Moses was a man well acquainted with the glory of God. Amazingly, the promise of the New Testament is that believers like you and I will see greater glory than Moses ever saw:

*"Now if the ministry that brought death, which was engraved in letters on stone, came with glory, so that the Israelites could not look steadily at the face of Moses because of its glory, transitory though it was, will not the ministry of the Spirit be even more glorious? If the ministry that brought condemnation was glorious, how much more glorious is the ministry that brings righteousness! For what was glorious has no glory now in comparison with the surpassing glory. And if what was transitory came with glory, how much greater is the glory of that which lasts!"* (2 Corinthians 3:7-11)

Moses saw the fire of God, heard the trumpets of heaven, knew supernatural provision as rocks burst forth water, and manna appeared on the ground six days a week. An entire nation's clothes did not wear out for decades. Every sick person leaving Egypt was healed. Incredible plagues destroyed their enemies. Moses' face shone with the glory of God to the point that the Israelites were compelled to cover it up! Yet the New Testament says, *"will not the ministry of the Spirit be even more glorious"* and *"how much greater is the glory of that which lasts!"*

There is an outpouring of glory, God's splendour and

goodness made visible, that is supposed to accompany the New Covenant, our relationship with Jesus Christ today. We know from the book of Acts that the early Church saw pillars of fire, loud noises from heaven, speaking in tongues, the dead raised and rooms shaken – but there is so much more to come! (Acts 2:2-13, 4:31, 9:40)

2 Corinthians 3:17-18 goes on to promise:

*"Now the Lord is the Spirit, and where the Spirit of the Lord is, there is freedom. And we all, who with unveiled faces contemplate the Lord's glory, are being transformed into His image with ever-increasing glory, which comes from the Lord, who is the Spirit."*

While the experience of Moses was a "fading glory", by contrast ours is called an EVER INCREASING GLORY! At some point in this journey on earth, we should be experiencing levels of glory and splendour that eclipse anything seen by Moses, David, Solomon, or any disciple in the Gospels and the book of Acts. That is an incredible thought!

> I believe, now is the commencement of that age
> – an age of glory in the Church.

## Glory in our Hearts

2 Corinthians 4:6 goes on to teach that,

*"God, who said, 'Let light shine out of darkness,' made His light shine in our hearts to give us the light of the knowledge of God's glory displayed in the face of Christ. But we have this*

*treasure in jars of clay to show that this all-surpassing power is from God and not from us.*"

No longer is the glory of God in a tent or a temple, the result being that Moses' "face-glory" faded once he walked away. No longer is His glory only in heaven. The veil is torn! (Luke 23:45). We now live in an age when God has taken the glory from the temple and has placed it in our hearts. Where we can behold Him face to face in prayer and devotion.

> **As we worship and enjoy Him in our hearts, our sense of His glory can increase, until His power and presence floods out across the earth.**

The pillar of cloud and fire that hung over the tabernacle and the tent of meeting, and which filled Solomon's temple, appeared again on the day of Pentecost. A fire appeared (Acts 2:3 was literally a pillar) and for the first time in history it split into 120 and rested over every head, signifying that *we*, the Church and temple of Christ, would now be the place of residence of the glory of God.

Over the last 500 years we have been reformed and restored. Great pockets of glory have been seen at different times throughout the ages. But now we are coming to the full measure of the mature stature of Christ. The fullness of God on the earth, resting on the grace-covered shoulders of the sons of God!

## The Call to Glory

The New Testament is ablaze with references to the ultimate result of our salvation being a sharing in the privilege of being glory carriers:

*"Now if we are children, then we are heirs—heirs of God and co-heirs with Christ, if indeed we share in His sufferings in order that we may also share in His glory."* (Romans 8:17)

*"He called you to this through our gospel, that you might share in the glory of our Lord Jesus Christ."* (2 Thessalonians 2:14)

*"To the elders among you, I appeal as a fellow elder and a witness of Christ's sufferings who also will share in the glory to be revealed."* (1 Peter 5:1)

*"I consider that our present sufferings are not worth comparing with the glory that will be revealed in us."* (Romans 8:18)

The Bible even speaks of our salvation being a work towards glory – that Jesus wishes to share His glory with us (shocking to some!). And Paul writes that we should seek glory:

*"I have given them the glory that You gave me, that they may be one as we are one"* (John 17:22)

*"To those who by persistence in doing good seek glory, honour and immortality, He will give eternal life."* (Romans 2:7)

*"To them God has chosen to make known among the Gentiles the glorious riches of this mystery, which is Christ in you, the hope of glory."* (Colossians 1:27)

*"He called you to this through our gospel, that you might share in the glory of our Lord Jesus Christ."* (2 Thessalonians 2:14)

*"If you are insulted because of the name of Christ, you are blessed, for the Spirit of glory and of God rests on you."* (1 Peter 4:14)

In Hebrews 2:10 the writer describes the work of the cross so beautifully in one simple, yet mindblowing phrase: *"In bringing many sons and daughters to glory…"*

The Bible also speaks of the last of the last days being a time of glory, announcing the return of Christ. I realise that our classic interpretation of this has often been to think of the end of the age being a sudden rapture moment. But what if the waves of glory accompanying the coming of Christ look a little different than we had imagined?

> **However you read it, the last of the last days will be days of glory:**

*"For the creation waits in eager expectation for the children of God to be revealed. For the creation was subjected to frustration, not by its own choice, but by the will of the one who subjected it, in hope that the creation itself will be liberated from its bondage to decay and brought into the freedom and glory of the children of God."* (Romans 8:19-21)

*"For the Son of Man is going to come in His Father's glory with His angels."* (Matthew 16:27)

*"When the Son of Man comes in his glory, and all the angels with Him, He will sit on his glorious throne."* (Matthew 25:31)

*"If anyone is ashamed of me and my words in this adulterous and sinful generation, the Son of Man will be ashamed*

*of them when he comes in His Father's glory with the holy angels."* (Mark 8:38)

*"At that time people will see the Son of Man coming in clouds with great power and glory."* (Mark 13:26)

It would seem that God's purpose is for us to, somehow, share in His glory. To know His glory. To reveal His glory. Perhaps even to revel in His glory! And there is no doubt, the last of the last days are to be days of the glory of Christ on the earth. We are all well acquainted with the iconic passage of Messianic promise in Isaiah 60. Perhaps we need to read it more slowly in the light of our discoveries about God's designs for glory on the earth:

*"Arise, shine, for your light has come,*
 *and the glory of the LORD rises upon you.*
*See, darkness covers the earth*
 *and thick darkness is over the peoples,*
*but the LORD rises upon you*
 *and His glory appears over you*
*Nations will come to your light,*
 *and kings to the brightness of your dawn.*
*"Lift up your eyes and look about you:*
 *All assemble and come to you;*
*your sons come from afar,*
 *and your daughters are carried on the hip.*
*Then you will look and be radiant,*
 *your heart will throb and swell with joy;*
*the wealth on the seas will be brought to you,*
 *to you the riches of the nations will come.*

34

*Herds of camels will cover your land,*
*young camels of Midian and Ephah.*
*And all from Sheba will come,*
*bearing gold and incense*
*and proclaiming the praise of the* LORD.
*All Kedar's flocks will be gathered to you,*
*the rams of Nebaioth will serve you;*
*they will be accepted as offerings on my altar,*
*and I will adorn my glorious temple."* (Isaiah 60:1-7)

## I Will Not Share My Glory

I realise some biblically astute Christians reading this will be pondering the words of Isaiah 42:8, where God clearly states, *"I am the* LORD; *that is my name! I will not yield my glory to another."*

Many Christians have been taught that God would *never* give His glory to man, or share it with him. In many senses this is absolutely true!

But the phrase here literally means, "I will not share my glory with *someone different to me* (another)". And that is true. He will not share His glory with sinners, the immoral, the untrusting, the pride-filled and egotistical.

But here's the fun part: now that we are "in Christ Jesus" we are no longer, by His grace, "another". Instead we are sons of God, cleansed by faith in His grace; part of His Kingdom. That is why the New Testament is ablaze with scriptures about God sharing His glory with us. We were sinners who had fallen short of God's glory, but we are justified freely by His grace (Romans 3:23) and made able to carry His glory once again! This is a divine work of His mercy.

Now let's look practically at how that might work, and what small part we play in knowing His glory…

## Jesus Died So We Could Be Glorified

What must we do with this incredible thought that the reformation of the last 500 years, ending with the restoration of apostle and prophets, means we are a completed (though still very imperfect!) temple, ready for the glory of God?

> If we are about to enter a new age of glory
> in the Church then what must we do?

This is so grand a theme, is there anything we *can* do?

Romans 3:23 states that, *"all have sinned and fall short of the glory of God"*, but wonderfully goes on to state that we are *"justified freely by His grace."*

The first thing I want to state (perhaps the only piece of advice I can bring!) is that this must be a work of grace. No one is holy enough, able enough, strong enough or devoted enough to earn God's glory on/in our lives. An Age of Glory will also have to be an Age of Grace. Here's why:

Romans 8:29-30 states,

*"For those God foreknew He also predestined to be conformed to the image of His Son, that He might be the firstborn among many brothers and sisters. And those He predestined, He also called; those He called, He also justified; those He justified, He also glorified."*

These verses teach us that God knows us, and He has predestined us to become like Jesus. He calls us, justifies us and glorifies us. These verses show us that we can relax about our development: God is fully committed to making us like Jesus and filling us with His glory. God has always planned to make you like Jesus. He always planned the Church would grow through the last 500 years of reformation, preparing us for this age of glory.

> The full weight of God's glory will rise upon us as it says in Isaiah 60, but it will be a work of grace.

## Justified Leads to Glorified

In between being called and being glorified there is a vital step. It is the word *justified*.

It is justification that leads to glorification. Without an understanding of justification we will never fully enter the realms of glory, of power, or of His awesome presence.

> Fully understanding the beauty and power of justification is possibly the one thing we should hold onto in this incredible time.

To be justified simply means to be "rendered as though we had never sinned". It is a work done by Christ's shed blood on the cross. It is to be righteous. To be clean. To be right with God and at peace with Him. Somehow, understanding this will lead to the availability of His glory in our lives.

Now, of course, this work was done by Jesus on the cross, but the more we fully accept the work of the cross, the more powerful our experience of His glory will be. In short, when we embrace His goodness, we will enjoy His glory.

> **Too many well-meaning, sincere Christians walk around with low-level residual guilt and shame...**

...a dullness that means they never quite feel fully right. They feel, "If only I could pray a little more, read the Bible a little more, fail a little less..." then surely they would be holy. But this goes against the work of the cross! The cross has declared that you are holy, you are righteous, you are justified, you are free from sin, you are loved fully by God just as you are as you turn to Him and trust Him.

Get your heart around these key scriptures regarding the work of Jesus on the cross:

*"For it is by grace you have been saved, through faith—and this is not from yourselves, it is the gift of God— not by works, so that no one can boast. For we are God's handiwork, created in Christ Jesus to do good works, which God prepared in advance for us to do."* (Ephesians 2:8-10)

*"Therefore, if anyone is in Christ, the new creation has come: The old has gone, the new is here! All this is from God, who reconciled us to Himself through Christ and gave us the ministry of reconciliation: that God was reconciling the world to Himself in Christ, not counting people's sins against them."* (2 Corinthians 5:17-19)

This glorious salvation is not a work born of yourself, it is simply something you must believe and receive. And the more you grasp it, are persuaded by it, the more you will approach the throne of grace by the blood of Jesus, confident and in full assurance of faith that He accepts you.

> *You don't have to try to be right with Him.*
> *You are already right with Him.*

## The Twisted Kiss

In Brennan Manning's masterpiece of a book *The Ragamuffin Gospel* he describes an event that perfectly exemplifies the work of the cross and the acceptance of Christ – the only route to glorification; the only way His glory can fill our lives by a work of magnificent grace.

Manning writes about a surgeon who has just operated on a young woman, whose face is now slightly deformed:

"I stand by the bed where a young woman lies, her face postoperative, her mouth twisted in palsy, somewhat clownish. A tiny twig of the facial nerve, the one to the muscles of her mouth, had been severed. She will be this way from now on.

I had followed with religious fervour the curve of her flesh; nevertheless, to remove the tumour in her cheek, I had to cut the little nerve.

Her young husband is in the room. He stands on the opposite side of the bed and together they seem to dwell in the evening lamplight, isolated from me; the moment is a private one.

Who are they, I ask myself? He and this wry mouth I have made, who gaze at each other so generously, so lovingly. The young woman speaks.

'Will my mouth always be like this?' she asks.

'Yes,' I say, 'it will. It is because the nerve was cut.'

She nods and is silent. But the young man smiles.

'I like it,' he says, 'It's kind of cute.'

All at once I know who he is. I understand and I lower my

gaze. One is not bold in an encounter with a God moment. Unmindful, he bends to kiss her crooked mouth and I am so close I can see how he twists his own lips to accommodate hers; to show her that their kiss still works."

Through the cross, God has twisted His kiss to fit our "crooked little mouths".

> He has made up the difference for our failure
> and brokenness through His blood.

So that even while we are growing in God, improving in Him, going from glory to glory, we can still say that we are fully holy, fully right with God, fully justified.

Hebrews 10:10 says, *"We have been made holy through the sacrifice of the body of Jesus Christ"* while verse 14 puts it this way: *"He has made perfect forever, those whose are being made holy".*

> It means we ARE HOLY and we are BEING MADE HOLY all at the
> same time. That is His grace! And God twists His kiss to
> accommodate our weakness.

I meet so many Christians that half believe this. They know it in theory, but actually they are still driven by guilt and self-improvement. It actually means they are flooded with self-righteousness when they are doing well, and become harsh and judgemental towards others. Then, when they behave in ways that are less than ideal, they are flooded with shame and an overwhelming sense of failure.

Whichever way you look at it, lives that don't grasp the grace of the cross are full of self – whether that is self-righteous judgmentalism or utter failure and shame.

Neither can be containers for God's glory, as both are based on fleshly strength and not the power and grace of God.

The better way is to fully accept and embrace the work of the cross:

> *To examine oneself less often, and spend much, much more time examining Jesus. Bathing in His presence, listening to His voice, obeying His whispers, being lost in worship and wonder and the weight of His presence.*

It is when we enter a lifestyle that utterly depends on the cross that sin is truly dealt with in our behaviour too. As we focus on His *"kindness that leads to repentance"* (Romans 2:4), and walk by the Spirit, we discover that all bondage and addictive behaviours fall away like autumn leaves from a tree.

## The Realisation of Grace

A little girl was born with a cleft pallet. Her self-esteem was deeply affected by the disfigurement. But, as a young girl, though deeply insecure, she had a teacher who truly adored her.

One day in class, the teacher ran an activity that was partly a hearing test, but also a fun game. Each pupil would stand in front of the class, with their back to the teacher. The teacher would whisper a phrase behind them, which they would then repeat if they could hear it.

To some of the little boys she whispered, "I want to be an astronaut" or "I love dirt."

To some of the girls she whispered, "I want to be a doctor" or "I love playing in the sun."

When it came to the turn of the little girl with the cleft palate, she walked out in front of the class and faced them nervously. Bending down to whisper just behind the ear of the little girl, the teacher quietly whispered, "I wish you were my little girl."

Like a fresh dawn, it was as though a fog of lies lifted. The bright light of truth entered her soul. She saw the truth with crystal clarity for the first time: "I am beautiful. Somebody loves me. Somebody wants me. I am precious."

That little girl grew up to say that this moment utterly transformed her life.

It's the same with you. God made you for one reason – to love you.

> *It's time you started letting Him love you, forgive you, make you at peace with Himself; to let Him fill your life with power, presence, intimacy and glory!*

The revelation of justification can be a moment of profound realisation when we finally grasp it. The mist of religious striving lifts as we realise for the first time how utterly precious we are; totally forgiven of all sins past, present and future. The blazing sun of mercy shines into our dulled hearts and we come alive. Alive to God's glory, as we realise we are fit for it by a work of grace! Alive to God's power as we sense the dignity of heaven filling us with the authority of Jesus. Awake to the face of Jesus as, for the first time, we realise He is so close, so accepting, so approving of us, even though we still carry areas of brokenness that are under construction.

> *When our hearts fully grasp that God is smiling upon us, we will be fit for glory.*

So I believe, and I humbly put before you dear reader, that the completion of 500 years of reformation, capped by the restoration of apostles and prophets, is bringing us, the Church, to the point at which we can begin to enter into the "full stature of Christ" in the earth. This will result in a sense of glory upon the Church, that she would be a City on a Hill that cannot be hidden, shining forth with God as her light.

This will mean you too, will know God's glory in increasing ways in your life.

But the only way we can walk in such glory is by a work of divine grace; a realisation that the cross was not only to forgive us and give us eternal assurance, but to glorify us to the point where we rule and reign in life in Him today.

In recent years the restored prophets of the Church have been announcing a new era, a new season, a new age. They speak with remarkable unity about a new chapter in Church history, which we will explore in the next chapter.

# Chapter Three
# A New Era Prophesied

Daniel 2: 21 states that God, *"changes times and seasons"* while Acts 17:26 says that God, *"determines pre-appointed times."* In addition, Amos 3:7 tells us that, *"Surely the Sovereign LORD does nothing without revealing His plan to His servants the prophets."* So we would expect a flow of new season announcements to begin to flood the newly restored ministry of the prophets if God is about to do some new thing.

Prophets in the Body of Christ are like the *"Sons of Issachar"* (1 Chronicles 12:32) – those who know and announce the times and seasons of heaven. As I've pored over prophetic words from around the world in recent times I have indeed found a recurring theme that a new era, a new age, a new Church chapter is emerging.

For what follows, I am indebted to the excellent compilation of historic prophetic words from around the world, collected with care at ElijahList.com and Richard-Watch.org

## Chuck Pierce

In November 2008 Chuck Pierce spoke of a vision: "I saw a

new move of God coming in England ... The Spirit of the Lord says to the people of England, 'This is your season for your light to come forth at night. You will shine in the midst of the night.'"

In 2012 he prophesied again: "I've been here many, many times and you can sense something beginning to change. You're entering a new day, a new era – a new Kingdom era."

Speaking over the little revivalist nation of Wales (my home country!) Chuck prophesied in September 2013:

"I say to you I am bringing a new quickening of power across Wales. Get ready, for a quickening power that will cause the birth of heaven to come down into the atmosphere of this nation, is now being released ... I say three generations will now arise in this land and see Me move in a new way. I say to you, I want to begin new and fresh ... An angelic host have been waiting, and many have come, but now they stand positioned in the land, ready to say who will go with Me into this season ahead."

## Clifford Hill

The message of a new season seems to have been washing like waves on our shores, well known prophetic figure Clifford Hill more tentatively mentioning, "The Lord has been speaking to me for some time about a 'new season' and a 'new message'. I've been growing in excitement, but I've not dared to say anything to anyone in case it's just been my imagination..."

## Dr Sharon Stone

In November 2012, Dr Sharon Stone, a proven prophetic minister based in Windsor, prophesied in the wake of hurricane Sandy, "The Lord kept saying that this hurricane and these winds are 'a punctuation' – not just in the US, but a punctuation in the world … These are re-arranging winds and they're changing the course of nations … Hidden winds of change have been developing on the inside of My people and they are now blowing change into the world."

Later Dr Sharon Stone prophesied, "We are in a season unlike anything I've ever lived in before – one where His glory is more readily available to us than at any time I've ever seen. And we're seeing more of His glory being poured out; we're hearing of more encounters with the presence of the Lord."

## John Kilpatrick / Stephen Herzig

In the United States Rev John Kilpatrick, most renowned for a move of revival in the 1990s stated, "The Lord said, 'Tell My people I have brought about a season change...'", while Stephen Herzig, from Christ Of The Nations, in September 2013 prophesied, "This is a time of 'new beginnings'. What 'was' is no more. What 'will be' needs new foundations" – signalling that a preparation time for a new era was underway.

## Roy Fields

Roy Fields, a US worship leader well acquainted with the atmosphere of revival prophesied in 2012, said, "I hear God saying this over the UK: 'It's been cloudy over the UK, but the sun is coming out, and the light is about to shine like never before in the darkness. And there shall be many that have fallen away that will come back' … The prodigals are going to return to the house of the Lord. Sickness and disease are going to be cast away. I see bars shutting down. I see drug addicts getting healed. I see marriages getting back together. I see the Church rising up in faith and power.

And I see the enemy taking a blow to the head. I see pastors coming back together, laying down all their walls of division. I see territories being done away with. I see different denominations and streams coming together to worship. I see priests and vicars and pastors. I'm telling you, I see this all over the UK. You may not believe it right now because of what you see, but I tell you, hear my voice. By the Spirit of the Lord, the Lord says, 'I want My body to be one.' Oh, hallelujah! I see Christians getting their passion back for the Gospel. I see people of God burying themselves in the Bible. I see the words of the scriptures of the Holy Bible coming alive in the hearts of the people. I see people rising up, full of the Holy Ghost, changing nations, changing cities, going into remote areas and taking dominion,"

## Charles Shamp

In 2014 Charles Shamp said, under the inspiration of the Holy Spirit, "There's coming to this country signs and wonders that this country's never seen before. We're birthing something that has never been in this country … This nation has seen mighty moves of revival, but the *latter* movement of the glory of God *that is coming now* over this nation is going to trump everything you've ever seen in the UK. It's *not* going to look like the old thing – it's *something completely brand new* and what it's going to do is literally even to shake ground in this country…"

## Cindy Jacobs

In January 2013 Cindy Jacobs stated, "…we are entering a new era. Things cannot be done in the same way they have in the past season. The new era is a 'But now' season…".

In 2014 Cindy Jacobs prophesied to the United Kingdom: "'I am coming to Wales, but not as I have done in times past, but …in a greater measure, for I never do anything lesser than what I did before. I am releasing a wave of Glory out of Scotland that will affect many nations,' says the Lord. 'For this is going to be a transformation that affects all of Europe and the nations of the earth. There is a new sound arising out of England unlike any that has been released before. I am calling my people to once again fill the streets with singing and dance upon injustice … I say that it is time for the Lion of Judah to roar upon this land… Wake up and call unto me!'"

## Heidi Baker

In 2014 Heidi Baker spoke of a great change emerging out of the United Kingdom: "'There's going to be a movement of unity in the UK that's going to shake the world,' says the Lord. I hear the prophetic word of the Lord. It's another wave of revival He's promised. This move of God is different than you've ever seen before … because no one's going to point to one mighty evangelist. There's going to be a move of unity within the Body of Christ … another historic move of God … you are going to come together for the prize … 'I will give you souls!'"

## Veronika West

Finally, Veronika West, prophesied in April 2016 a, "sudden supernatural shift happening in the realms of the Spirit in this hour. *Get ready* for there is an emerging army of mighty warriors coming forth from a firestorm of glory. Watch!!! For the manifestation of greater signs, wonders and miracles!"

## Days of Wonder

Over and over again the prophets are speaking of a changing season, a new era, a greater day and the dawning of a new age. In January 2013 the UK Prophetic Council released a word concluding that we are, "moving into an historic season to be known as 'Days of Wonder.'"

This particular phrase is dear to my heart, as in 1996 God gave me a vision of revival, calling it the "Days of Wonder". I had been flying from London on a flight that appeared to be stopping at every African village en-route to Johannesburg. Sleeping through the night I was wakened by a startling vision of the glory of God. I lay terrified for several minutes, then slipped back into sleep. On arrival in South Africa the visions continued for several nights. Whilst ministering in South Africa God began to move at a level I had seldom seen before. People were healed, saved; drug addicts overwhelmed by the power of God. There were sightings of angels, visions of the future, and whole congregations were taken up into wondrous meetings with God. Backsliders came back to Christ, the oppressed were delivered, the unsaved fell down, overcome by God's presence and got up saved! It was amazing.

Accompanying the powerful times of ministry was an overwhelming sense of vision for the future. I now believe these were visions of the coming age – of the glory of the Lord beginning to cover the earth as the waters cover the sea.

# Chapter Four
# Glory Breaking Forth

I wrote more about the vision described at the end of the previous chapter in my book, *Glory in the Church*. It was my first vision of glory:

"In 1996 I encountered the glory of God in a six-week visit to South Africa. During that time I was filled with a vision for the United Kingdom and Europe. Night after night I awoke, day after day I prayed, and visions of a great revival were burned into my heart. I am convinced the Church must be ready to host a glory at a level previously unknown. The presence of God is preparing to sweep across Europe as never seen before. It will be in response to the apostolic reformation currently underway. Stadiums, arenas and the greatest auditoriums will be turned into church buildings. Marketplaces, filled with thousands, will be overcome by the glory of God. The blind will see. The lame will walk. Street evangelism will happen as never before, as mass healings take place on street corners and in shopping centres. Where many have spent years sowing, others will reap on a massive scale.

God's glory will touch the media, politics and royalty. His glory will invade live TV shows, as men and women of God reveal the power of God in healings, strange signs and prophetic words and wisdom. Many politicians will come to Christ in a very visible way. For some this will bring prominence, for others ridicule and scandal. Governments and kings will call days of prayer. Thousands will stream into the Kingdom of God as a great move of signs and wonders floods our churches, workplaces and homes.

Some believers will be transfigured as Moses was. Trances, dreams and visions will become commonplace. The weather will be controlled by believers at certain times, and used as a sign to communities where they are ministering. Neighbours will knock on the doors of those known to be Christians, begging to be led to Christ and to find peace for their souls. Many businesses and workplaces will hold prayer meetings; some will even close for whole days of prayer. Study groups will meet at all hours of the day in business establishments.

The glory of God will fill the greatest auditoriums in the land as Christians try to find places to gather that can contain the numbers flooding into the Kingdom. Great and glorious signs and wonders will be performed by apostolic teams, though even the least among the Church will see miracles as commonplace. Churches will be planted on a daily basis. Leaders will be trained quickly and released easily. Youngsters will lead churches of thousands. A softening of hearts between generations in churches will mean all ages will worship and walk together."

Since 1996, when I received this original vision, some of it has begun to come to pass. There have been remarkable stadium events, waves of the glory of God, and salvations and miracles on the streets. As I have continued to dwell and ponder prophetically on the themes of God's coming glory to the world, the original vision has become full colour, panoramic and 3D!

I realise that prophetic visions can only ever be a "seeing in part" – it's just a part of the picture (1 Corinthians 13:9,12). They can also sound overly idealistic and Utopian to the realists amongst us. We must remember that even during God's greatest moves people still sin, argue, endure struggles and have to wear deodorant! All is not rosy or easy. Revival does not, in reality, feel like its stories sound.

> But I believe God often shows us perfect prophetic pictures on the mountain of His presence, to help us endure the valley of development with determination.

Please keep this in mind as you read the next section. Today I would add the following prophetic observations in my original visions of 1996:

## Glory upon the Church

The Church will be filled with glory. A weighty sense of presence that has grown since the early 1900s will begin to flood every corner of the Church. Even the most stoic of Church expressions will be found weeping at the wonder of His goodness again. Of course, there will be a backlash – that the coming glory is a figment of overly excited "Charismatic" imaginations. But the rising tide of glory and power will reach everyone who is thirsty. The coming move will be so obviously brought by the hand of heaven, that most of the Church will eventually open itself to new realms of power.

The Catholic and even other more "High" traditions will begin to be influenced powerfully by a new presence from heaven.

> The beauty of history and liturgy will blend with presence and glory in ways many Pentecostals and Charismatics have thought impossible – and glory will rise upon the most historic of churches.

The Church will become more of a movement and less of a club for members. She will pour out into the streets and the various strata of society, invading the very fabric of communities. She will meet in buildings large and small, facilitated by new types of church governmental structures that are fluid, relational, releasing and non-bureaucratic.

Denominationalism will give way to Kingdom authority, led by servant apostles. Different streams or tribes in the Church will no longer be seen as competition, or lacking doctrinal accuracy. Instead, each tribe in the Kingdom will bring fresh emphasis, a strength that the whole Body of Christ needs. New authority structures will create Kingdom flow that lacks bureaucracy and releases the Saints to march across the land in power.

> Church unity will flow as never before – such will be the harvest of souls.

There will simply be too many people being saved to worry about the politics of pastoring. No longer will pastors fight over members. They will send each other members when their discipleship systems become overwhelmed by the sheer numbers.

Signs and wonders will become incredibly commonplace – even among children and denominations formerly thought of as "dead". Indeed, the dead will be raised, remarkable healings and miracles occur. There will be transfigurations – men and women glowing with the presence of God. Some will be lifted off the ground, objects will move, the smoke of glory will fill streets, rooms, stadiums, parliaments. It will rain indoors. Even oil will flow in miraculous ways. The wonders will cause worship to God and become so commonplace in certain locations, that they even seem to no longer fascinate the believers.

But these signs will fascinate the world and eventually be impossible to ignore, even by the most wary of media outlets.

## Politics and Government

God said, "My glory will invade politics, carried on the shoulders of the ambassadors of heaven. Men and women, who have met me in my glory, will be given the opportunity and mantle to stand for office and call my presence in.

Prayer meetings will run like rivers through parliament buildings. The EU will become engulfed in a war for its soul, as the Kingdom of light begins to penetrate even the darkest corners."

"The war for power in the boardrooms and cabinet rooms of the world will rage, but a new grace from my hand, that seems to melt even the greatest authorities will begin to invade meetings and conversations," God says.

While some have felt that an Elijah-like confrontation will be the event that turns men of power around, it will actually be a release of softening grace that will melt the hearts of kings and presidents. This is the age of grace and glory. Favour from the hand of God and man will be released in the earth, and the Church will be established as prince among the mountains.

> The rise of a new type of missionary from the Church will begin to transform politics locally.

Strong, spiritual, biblically literate and fearless, the Church will march into the political arena ready to be a city on a hill.

## Media and the Arts

The Church will become known again as a womb of creativity for art, music, words and media. Christian artists will be recognised as the source of immense creative expertise, as training schools in the arts arise in every city, nation and continent.

Film-makers will send shockwaves throughout the world, explaining the fallen brokenness of man, melting the hardness of pride and releasing a longing for divine grace and healing.

> It is the arts, not politics, that will touch and reshape the morality of nations back into the image of God.

Through stories, song, and the retelling of divine history, the arts will capture the hearts of humanity and make many question the moral anarchy that has swept the world.

Stadiums will be used for church services again and again. The greatest auditoriums in the land will be filled. The arts and signs and wonders will run like streams, blending into a river of grace and glory that will capture the hearts of millions. Kings, presidents, the influencers of the world, will weep in worship at the presence of God. Royalty will fall prostrate before the Father's presence.

> *Revivals will accompany theatre companies. Anointed productions will be performed that lead the audience to an overwhelming travailing of the soul.*

Queues will go on endlessly as people long to be in God's presence and hear the words once again. Audience members will convulse in their seats, cry out, rush the stage, run out to the streets, overcome by the Holy Spirit's presence, in deep repentance. Some will be left overnight in the theatre as the glory of God moves and crowds become immobile under the hand of God's glory. In some areas this will become considered a normal response to the arts, such will be the power and anointing of God at work.

Successful, renowned singers will begin to turn their concerts into evangelistic campaigns – even giving away Bibles, taking altar calls, and working with local churches. In some great auditoriums, multiple celebrities will give testimony and perform, with thousands giving their lives to Christ and leaving new churches planted.

Small radio stations will spring up across the earth broadcasting the Gospel, proclaiming the power and presence of God, telling salvation stories, releasing the testimonies of communities in regional areas. They will become the new pulpits of the airwaves. Thousands will be healed simply by listening, as the wisdom and wonder of God floods the airwaves. Some of these places will become so successful that larger stations will model themselves on the pattern of these glory stations.

## Glory Invading Education

Schools, colleges and universities will be in upheaval at the moves of revival. Christian unions will hold prayer meetings that fill up like assemblies. Outpourings of the Spirit will interrupt classes. Teachers will, at times, become preachers, as God's presence moves so strongly in their classrooms. Many will fall to the floor overcome by God's presence.

> Great wars will be fought around the classrooms, as the enemy vies for the minds of the young, but the glory of God will prevail.

Schools, colleges and universities will be swept up in visitations of glory so strong that head teachers will be unable to finish prayers and speeches as they weep under the hand of God, and the young people assembled begin to sing under the infilling of the Spirit.

"Missionary" will become a common recommendation for careers advice. The hunger for millions to carry God's glory to the ends of the earth will grow as the compulsion of love drives a new generation to invade every last corner of the earth with the Gospel.

## God and Medicine

God's glory will empty some hospitals. Saints will go in and prayer will fast become another normalised route to wellness. There will be many times when wards are emptied by the visit of a group of *glory carriers*.

But what is more remarkable is that it will become acceptable again for doctors to pray and lay hands on the sick. They will see the dead raised, intensive care patients radically healed, and many will come to faith in hospital.

In many places, prayer will become an activity accepted, taught, and recommended as a legitimate means of healing. Some medical universities will specialise in prayer for healing, helping to release an army of "divine doctors" able to walk in miracles and medicine.

Some hospitals will develop "miracle teams" who are trained and released to move around the hospitals praying, caring and comforting the sick. Churches will be set up in hospital wings.

## God and the Family

The make-up of the family will be restored, not by the laws of man, but by a movement of grace upon the broken hearts of humanity.

> *The oil of God's grace will flow upon the earth, and through encounter after encounter the hearts of humanity, so hungry for approval and acceptance, will be restored to the Father's Heart.*

There will be outpost after outpost, where a restoration of families will become the norm. Divorce will drastically reduce, fatherlessness will fade, sexual confusion will give way to peace and holiness.

In some places it will be the Church family that become the "father and mother" of communities, bringing stability, nourishment, approval, discipline and tenderness. The Church will seem, in some places, to be almost a parental figure in the nation, rather than an irrelevant relic. Adoption and fostering ministries will explode across church communities, as God sets the lonely in healthy families.

## God's Glory on Businesses and Financial Institutions

Businessmen will be touched powerfully by glory and become Generals of Commerce, releasing finances and resources into the global harvest. But not only will they resource ministries and churches, their very businesses will become strongholds of the Kingdom, bringing societal transformation and change.

Godly business men and women will be seen as spiritual elders in the cities, and many will run churches alongside, and even within, their businesses and staff. A commitment to transforming a city or region will mean businesses become places of Kingdom rulership, to better advance the glory of God across and area.

> The glory of God will disrupt the business day again and again!

Some leaders will have to trust that everything will get done and profits will be made, as some will give up days to prayer and seeking God, allowing their staff to remain in God's presence, rather than being on "the production line." But these businesses will prosper greatly in God's hand, bringing wealth and influence for the Kingdom.

## Glory Across the Earth

Habakkuk 2:14 states that,

> *"The knowledge of the glory of the Lord is going to cover the earth as the waters cover the sea."*

If the knowledge of the glory of the Lord is going to cover the earth like the seas, then that may mean there will be vast areas of glory, but also places where the glory is held back for a time.

60

Just as the seas are held back by the land, so the earth will be divided by great portions that accept the outpouring of glory, but zones where it seems as though hell and destruction are at work even more powerfully than ever. These are the final death throes of the enemy's work on the earth.

> **Slowly though, God's glory will invade the whole earth,
> until she is covered evenly, deeply, and overwhelmed
> by a growing tide of glory and grace.**

God's presence will seem to hover over entire cities. An unusual atmosphere, sometimes of sombre conviction, and at other times of great joy, will seem to pervade the streets and businesses.

Mass evangelism – something some have thought to be a thing of the past – will become widespread, as crowds fill auditoriums, stadiums, arenas, fields and city centres. Worship will go on for hours. Many thousands will be overcome by the strong presence of God. Miracles and manifestations of the Spirit will take place – sometimes "performed" by believers, and at other times, simply by the hand of God on a city.

* * *

Some years ago, whilst pondering all these visions and dreams, I wrote a song called *Glory in the Land*. In it, I imagine being in my 90s, looking back at a world touched by glory. Perhaps you too, might reminisce with me one day:

*Do you remember what we saw,*
*When the glory of the Lord*
*Hung like fire in our skies,*
*And the nation began to cry?*

*Do you remember in the streets,*
*When His love brought thousands to their knees*
*And in the marketplace people cried,*
*Overwhelmed by mercy from on high?*

*Do you remember how it was,*
*When heavens fire fell on Londons lost*
*And people wandered at times for days,*
*Crying out, "How can I be saved?"*

*He shone like fire in the sky,*
*And His glory captured every eye.*
*The sun like darkness, the moon like blood...*
*There was glory, glory in the land.*
*There was glory, glory in the land.*

# Chapter Five
## Prophesies of a New Age

A last days era of glory has been prophesied by many, particularly over the last 100 or so years. The US prophet Bill Hamon once called it, "God's World War 3". In that prophetic word he stated,

"The Church has now entered God's World War 3. For God to have a third world war, He had to have a first and second. God's WWI was fought to produce the First Reformation of the Church. God sent His Commander-in-Chief of the armies of Heaven to earth as a human baby. He grew to a man, and at the age of 30, Jesus launched His campaign.

The war was to destroy the works of the devil and provide redemption for mankind. Jesus fought His first battle with the devil at the temptation in the wilderness. Father God then anointed Jesus with the Holy Spirit and power, as He went about destroying the works of the devil by healing people of their devilish afflictions and casting Satan's demons out of people.

Jesus' winning battle was on the cross, where He provided redemption for mankind. Then, by His resurrection from the dead, He took the keys of death and hell from the devil. Jesus then birthed His Church and gave His Church power and authority over the devil and all his demons. Thereby WWI was won.

God's World War 2 began in 1517 at the beginning of the 2nd Reformation, which was for the purpose of restoring all truth and ministries back to being active in the Church. The first shot was fired when God's General Martin Luther nailed his 95 Theses to the door of his Church in Wittenberg, Germany.

It took many battle-restoration movements over 490 years to retake all the truths and ministries that the devil had captured during the 1,000 year Dark Age of the Church. Most of them were restored back into the Church by the end of 2007. Thereby, God's World War 2 was won and the Second Reformation of the Church was fulfilled."

He goes on to say that NOW is declared God's World War 3, "...when the 3rd and Final Church Reformation is birthed in the Church." He continues,

> "The next great move of God is the manifest Army of the Lord. It will produce the most manifestations of God's power and glory ever recorded in Church history...

...It will continue until the glory of the Lord fills the earth as the waters cover the sea." (Numbers 14:21; Habakkuk 2:14).[1]

\* \* \*

For a century God's men and women have prophesied – regardless of their exact wording or personal theological slant – about an era of glory, or heightened presence and power, that would engulf the world.

In 1909, Charles Parham, father of the Pentecostal movement, and William Seymour, leader of the Azusa Street Revival, received virtually identical revelations without collaboration. One was on the east coast and the other on the west coast. They hadn't been in touch beforehand. Both leaders said that in about 100 years there would come an even greater revival which would be like the former and latter rains coming at the same time. They also said it wouldn't just be a relatively local outpouring, like at Azusa Street, but it would be all over the world! [2]

In my book *When Spirit & Word Collide*, I discuss the implications of an important prophetic word for the United Kingdom and Europe that many attribute to Smith Wigglesworth. In 1947 he prophesied:

"During the next few decades there will be two distinct moves of the Holy Spirit across the Church in Great Britain. The first move will affect every church that is open to receive it, and will be characterised by a restoration of the baptism and gifts of the Holy Spirit.

The second move of the Holy Spirit will result in people leaving historic churches and planting new churches.

In the duration of each of these moves, the people who are involved will say, 'This is a great revival.' But the Lord says, 'No, neither is this the great revival, but both are steps towards it.'"

> The amazing reality is that these moves have all taken place, which means we are poised to be the generation that experience this new, great era of God's moving.

Wigglesworth continued:

"When the new church phase is on the wane, there will be evidence in the churches of something that has not been seen before: a coming together of those with an emphasis on the Word and those with an emphasis on the Spirit. When the Word and the Spirit come together, there will be the biggest move of the Holy Spirit that the nation, and indeed the world, has ever seen. It will mark the beginning of a revival that will eclipse anything that has been witnessed within these shores, even the Wesleyan and Welsh revivals of former years. The outpouring of God's Spirit will flow over from the United Kingdom to mainland Europe and, from there, will begin a missionary move to the ends of the earth."[3]

At another time, the Apostle Smith Wigglesworth cried as he spoke to Lester Sumrall, saying, "I probably won't see you again now. My job is almost finished." As he continued to pray, he cried, "I see it, I see it!"

Dr Sumrall asked, "What do you see, what do you see?

Apostle Wigglesworth said, "I see a healing revival coming right after World War II. It'll be so easy to get people healed. I see it! I see it! I won't be here for it, but you will be." And there indeed was a healing revival right after the war.

Apostle Wigglesworth continued to prophesy, "I see another one. I see people of all different denominations being filled with the Holy Ghost." That was the Charismatic Revival. God raised up people during that era.

Then Apostle Wigglesworth said, "I see another move of God. I see auditoriums full of people, coming with notebooks. There will be a wave of teaching on faith and healing." We did experience that wave he saw, and we call it the Word of Faith movement.

Apostle Wigglesworth then prophesied, "After that, after the third wave," he started sobbing, "I see the last day revival that's going to usher in the precious fruit of the earth. It will be the greatest revival this world has ever seen! It's going to be a wave of the gifts of the Spirit. The ministry gifts will be flowing on this planet earth. I see hospitals being emptied out, and they will bring the sick to the churches where they allow the Holy Ghost to move."[4]

Another time, Smith said to Sumrall that, "there would be untold numbers of uncountable multitudes that would be saved. No man will say 'so many, so many,' because nobody will be able to count those who come to Jesus. No disease will be able to stand before God's people… It will be a worldwide situation, not local," he said, "a worldwide thrust of God's power and God's anointing upon mankind." Then he opened his eyes and looked at me and said, "I will not see it, but you shall see it. The Lord says that I must go on to my reward, but that you will see the mighty works that He will do upon the earth in the last days."

I believe it was Lester Sumrall that once said, "The stadiums of the world are reserved for the last great breath of God" in the knowledge that stadiums would be filled with millions responding to the Gospel. Was he seeing the age of glory?

## The Glorious Last Hour – Tommy Hicks

It was on 25th July 1961 that Tommy Hicks saw in a vision "people that He (God) had anointed – hundreds of thousands of people all over the world – in Africa, Asia, Russia, China, America – all over the world. The anointing of God was upon these people as they went forth in the Name of the Lord. I saw these men and women as they went forth. They were ditch diggers; they were washerwomen; they were rich men; they were poor men. I saw people who were bound with paralysis and sickness, and blindness and deafness. As the

Lord stretched forth His hand to give them the anointing, they became well; they became healed, and they went forth. And this is the miracle of it. This is the glorious miracle of it:

> Those people would stretch forth their hand exactly as the Lord did, and it seemed that there was this same liquid fire that seemed to be in their hand.

As they stretched forth their hand they said, 'According to my word, be thou made whole.'

As these people continued in this mighty, end-time ministry, I did not fully realise what it was. And I looked to the Lord and said, 'What is the meaning of this?' And He said, 'This is that, that I will do in the last days. I will restore all that the cankerworm, the palmerworm, the caterpillar – I will restore all that they have destroyed. This, My people in the end-time, shall go forth; as a mighty army they will sweep over the face of the earth.'

As I was at a great height, I watched these people as they were going to and fro over the face of the earth. Suddenly there was a man in Africa, and in a moment he was transported in the Spirit of God, and perhaps he was in Russia, or China, or America, or some other place, and vice versa; all over the world these people went. And they came through fire and through pestilence and through famine. Neither fire nor persecution – nothing seemed to stop them. Angry mobs came to them with swords and with guns, and like Jesus, they passed through the multitude and they could not find them. But they went forth in the Name of the Lord, and everywhere they stretched forth their hand the sick were healed, the blind eyes were opened. There was no long prayer.

And one of the things that seemed – after I had reviewed the vision so many times in my mind; and I thought about it so many times – I never saw a church, and I never saw or heard a denomination; but these people were going in the Name of the Lord of hosts. Hallelujah! As they marched forward, everything they did as the ministry of Christ, in the end-time. These people were ministering to the multitudes over the face of the earth. Tens of thousands, even millions, seemed to come to the Lord Jesus Christ as these people stood forth and gave the message of the Kingdom – of a coming Kingdom – in this last hour. It was so glorious.

> God is going to give to the world a demonstration in this last hour such as the world has never known.

These men and women are of all walks of life. Degrees will mean nothing. I saw these workers as they were going forth over the face of the earth. When one would seem to stumble and fall another would come and pick them up. There was no big 'I' and little 'You', but every mountain was brought low and every valley was exalted, and they seemed to have one thing in common: there was divine love that seemed to flow forth from these people as they went together, as they worked together, as they lived together. It was the most glorious thing that I have ever known. Jesus Christ was the theme of their life.

As I watched from the very heaven itself, there were times when great deluges of this liquid light seemed to fall upon great congregations. And that congregation would lift their hands and seemingly praise God for hours and even days as the Spirit of God came upon them. God said, 'I will pour My

Spirit upon all flesh,' and that is exactly the thing that God was doing; and to every man and to every woman that received this power and the anointing of God; the miracles of God – there was no ending to it."[5]

## Jean Darnell's Vision of the United Kingdom and Europe

Probably one of the most well known prophesys over Great Britain and Europe came from Jean Darnell in 1967:

"A vision came to me. It appeared three different times, during prayer, and it was the same vision each time. And what I saw was the British Isles, as in a bird's eye view. A kind of haze was over the whole, like a green fog. And then little pinpricks of light began to appear from the top of Scotland to Land's End. Then the Lord seemed to draw me closer to these lights, and I saw that they were fires that were burning. They were multiplying from the top of Scotland to Land's End. Then I saw lightning come and strike those fires, the brightest spots particularly, and there was a kind of explosion, and rivers of fire flowed down. Again, the sense of direction was from the top of Scotland to Land's End. But some of those rivers of fire didn't stop there. They went right across the Channel and didn't stop there. They went right across the Channel and spread out into the Continent.

> The Lord impressed it on my heart that those fires I saw were groups of people whom He would make intensely hungry for New Testament Christianity.

They would start reading their Bibles and saying, for instance, as they read the book of Acts, 'Well, where is this happy church? Where are these people so full of the power of the Holy Spirit?

Where are these miracles? Where is this growth, this vitality, this courage, this boldness that these people had? Is that for today – can we have it today? Should the Church be this way?'

And as these questions were being planted in their hearts, the Lord Jesus said He would make them very hungry for the Holy Spirit; He would fill them with the Holy Spirit, and out of those gifts would flow ministries that would enrich the Body of Christ. The whole concept of the Body of Christ would come alive, and barriers between denominations and different types of Christians would break down as people met each other. The Lord said He would move these people all over the country. After He had taught them gifts, He would move them to another place where they would carry that fire, and where they would meet others also who were being renewed by the Holy Spirit. He would put them in different situations from what they were used to, so that they would get to know people of other denominations, other cultures and other classes, and be able to communicate to them the blessings that the Lord had given them. And then He told me that during that time He would also test them. There would be great testing of faith, great waiting times. He would teach them spiritual warfare. He would show them the meaning of the power of the blood of Jesus, the name of Jesus, the Word of God and the power of the Holy Spirit.

Then I asked the Lord, 'What does the lightning stand for?' And He said, 'Unlike the first part, in which I will be speaking to Christians and preparing My Church and renewing it and reviving the saints, the lightning represents a second part of the vision, in which I will bring a spiritual awakening to the nation that will be a witness to the unsaved, to the un-churched, to the non-Christian.

Through these believers I will bring a witness to this land. They will be an army of witnesses. And I will begin to release their ministries, so that when they give their testimonies there will be apostolic signs following and accompanying their testimonies. Where ears have been deaf and hearts have been hard and eyes have been blind, I will touch the people of this land and they will begin to hear the testimony of My people; they will begin to see the manifestations of My power, and their hearts will begin to believe.

> Thousands and thousands of people are going to come into My Kingdom through this army of witnesses, through this people movement...

...not characterised by any particular evangelist or great organisation at the front, but just My people rising up, led by My Spirit and beginning to move forward with a new faith for evangelism, a new zeal to share Jesus with others. And as they give their testimonies, I will release their ministries of healing and miracles, and there will be signs and wonders accompanying their ministries. So many people will be saved, in the villages as well as in the cities, in the schools, in the government, in media, in industry. It will affect the destiny of this nation; it will determine the course of the times.

Then I said, 'Lord, what about these streams that go on across the Channel into Europe?' And He said, 'That represents people who will rise up in the midst of this people movement, this army of witnesses in Britain, whom I will make My communicators.' Now I hadn't used that word very much before in ministry, I said, 'Lord, what do you mean by communicators?' And he said, 'They will not only be people endowed with the gifts of the Holy Spirit, with strong faith, but they will also be people talented in the arts. They will be writers, musicians, singers and actors, and also technicians in television, radio and the mass media. I will call and send them and put them in strategic places. I will bless their natural talents with my Spirit, and they will be good: they will excel. They will be leaders in their fields. I will send them into Europe, where they will meet other people in the media, and through them I will release the word of God very fast in Europe. The result will be another wave of a spiritual awakening, with thousands coming to Christ throughout Europe.'[6]

In 1987 David Minor wrote, "'You have longed for revival and a return of the miraculous and the supernatural. You and your generation shall see it, but it shall only come by My process,' says the Lord. 'The church of this nation (the US) cannot contain My power in its present form. But as it turns to the wind of Holiness unto the Lord, it shall be purged and changed to contain my Glory. This is the judgment that has begun to the house of God, but it is not the end. When the second wind has come and brought in My harvest, then the end shall come.'"[7]

In 1989 Michael Backholer saw flames of fire appearing hundreds of feet high, flowing across a bridge from north to south. In astonishment he said, "What is it Lord?" having never received a vision before. "It's flames of revival. I'm going to send revival and it will start in the north and flow south," replied the Lord. "When will it come?" asked Michael, "Very soon," said the Lord. In 2004 God said to him, "I shall send a visitation of My power, the power of the Holy Spirit, to turn the hearts of the people away from sin to My Son. Millions, yes millions will be saved and swept into My Kingdom, for My glory and I shall empower them in these last days and they shall fan out as an army of witnesses, sharing the good news, all over this nation, including the islands offshore and I shall confirm My word with signs and wonders following them.

> *There will be miracles and healings in abundance, and out of this visitation I shall form a chain of grace that will reach across the Channel into Europe...*

...and to the nations of the world, and there will be a great harvest, an end-time harvest in preparation for Jesus' second coming."[8]

In 1992 Keith Powell said, "The Lord showed me a wave, a white waterfall moving unstoppably, powerfully, across the UK from the South West to the North East. As it moved over very, very slowly, but powerfully, it left a white, pure white cross across the UK and I asked the Lord, 'What's going on?' He said, 'I'm going to revive my Church and renew the nation and that symbolic white cross is a Holy Church, and a Holy Church will impact the nation.'"[9]

In 2012, the late Kim Clement prophesied, "'England, the United Kingdom shall never be the same again ... There is a sound that has been kept,' says the Spirit of God, 'even for this hour. It has been hidden and it has been covered, but,' God said, 'it's about to be opened up to a generation who are crying out. We have had a famine of hearing. We cannot hear; we do not want to hear. But that famine of hearing has come to an end. Young men and women will cry out and say, "We want to hear the sound. We want to hear the sound of life. We want to hear the sound of light. We want the infilling of the Spirit."' And God said, 'It shall not be as in the 1948 revival; this shall be the freshest, the newest thing that I shall do. They shall stand and watch it on their screens and through the screen I will touch them. They will feel the tangible presence of God coming through the screen, coming through the screen. And they will say, "We want it." And the Spirit of God will fill you and fill this generation and they will shout the name of Jesus from north to south and from east to west."[10]

In 2016 Dr Jerry Savelle prophesied, "More and more notable miracles will break loose in the earth. More and more signs and wonders. More and more angelic visitations. More and more instant healings. More and more deliverances from demonic activity. And, more and more finances will break loose, so My people can do more for the Kingdom of God."[11]

## The Song of Heaven Over the UK and USA

Charles Shamp has prophesied, "The Lion must roar before the Eagle can fly! I was shown in a vision a lion and an eagle. I then saw as the lion roared, the eagle took flight. The lion spoke to me of Great Britain and the roar of the Lord over the land – a roar of freedom and revival. The eagle taking flight spoke to me of America and her receiving freedom and awakening as a result of what would take place in Great Britain.

When we study the history of revival in the earth over the past several centuries, we can almost single handedly point to the United Kingdom as a major hot spot and catalyst for what the Holy Spirit was doing at that time. Almost every major shift of reformation or revival started on these Island Nations.

Whether we are discussing the First and Second Great Awakenings, or go further back and discuss the mystics and Catholic miracle workers that walked the shores of England, Ireland, Scotland, or Wales – God has always seemed to release the fresh movement of the Holy Spirit on these Islands that has gone on to affect the entire earth.

My love for Church history and the moves of the Spirit caused me to recognise that what took place within these nations directly affected America and the move of the Spirit in my nation. Although we are an ocean away, we are connected in the realm of the Spirit, and as the song of Heaven would arise over the UK, it would carry all the way to the shores of America and revival would begin to come forth in these United States."[12]

In January 2016 John Kilpatrick prophesied, "There is coming a great international harvest of souls through 'the net' (Internet) and 'online'. (The Lord) said that the Internet will light up as Holy Spirit accelerates His mighty wonders. He also said that 'the net' and 'lines' will bring tremendous and miraculous provision to God's people, because time is of the essence, and the waters are abundant for harvest. A new and very powerful wind of anointing will blow through the Internet. In real time, signs and wonders will be witnessed without edit. The heavens declare the glory of God, and the firmament will show forth His handiwork!"[13]

Also, in January 2016, Doug Addison prophesied that "glory is returning like never before."[14]

In February that year, Bobby Conner said we should, "Behold the Lamb in His Glory!" He went on, "These are days of destiny, filled with wonder and excitement. The awe of God is returning to the people of God, filling the heart of God's people with great expectation. Something new and revolutionary is at the door – but the question is not what is at the door, but Who. A cry for the manifest Presence of God is about to be answered. Every eye shall behold His brilliance and magnificent Glory and every veil shall be removed in order to behold the Lamb in His Glory. Indeed, much will be discovered in these revelatory days concerning the Glory of God and the God of Glory. Now is the time for every child of God to behold the Lord Jesus in His revealed Glory. The Word of God plainly declares that the entire earth will be filled with the knowledge of the Glory of God."[15]

Veronika West put it this way: "In the early hours, I had a powerful prophetic encounter that I would like to share with you. I ask that you read carefully and prayerfully, there is a sudden supernatural shift happening in the realms of the Spirit in this hour. Get ready, for there is an emerging army of mighty warriors coming forth from a firestorm of glory! Watch, for the manifestation of greater signs, wonders and miracles!"[16]

## The Glory of the Lion of Judah Shall Return

Finally, and worth noting at length, is a word that in 2005, Wendy Alec, co-founder of GOD TV, released via several media outlets:

"Oh, Great Britain, Great Britain – Isle of walls and of fortresses – I tell you that even as the glory of the Lord has departed from the Lion, so the glory of the Lion of Judah shall return – and My glory shall rest upon the Lion and the Lion once again shall open its mouth and its roar shall be heard again among the nations of this earth.

For even as in times past, the Lion whelped many, many cubs and sent its missionaries even to the uttermost parts of the earth, so I tell you that the glory of these latter days shall be greater than that of the former ... So I tell you, beloved, that in the decades to come, a great mobilising of My called out ones shall occur – of men and women and boys and girls from these shores – those who even slumber at this time shall start to arise,' says the Lord.

'For even as many of My children – even as much of My Church in Great Britain slumbers even this day – so I declare that I am about to blow the trumpet,' says the Lord, 'Yes, I the Lord God of Hosts am about to blow the trumpet in Zion and it shall resound with a mighty roar from the heavens, and My glory shall start to fall, and My Church and My called out ones shall rouse themselves from their stupor and from their slumber,' says the Lord.

'For even now I have heard the prayers of My people. Even now, although it be but a remnant, I have heard the prayers of the watchmen on the walls of Great Britain – the watchmen who neither slumber nor sleep – and even as they have cried out to me in the midnight hour for Britain to heed My voice and to seek My face, so I tell you My children, that the day of the Lord is appearing. And they shall rise from the East and from the West of this Isle; they shall rise from the Southernmost tip to the North, and Scotland – yes Scotland,' says the Lord.

'Yes, My burning fire shall be ignited in the furthermost parts of the North and My glory shall light a flame,' says the Lord, 'that shall sweep across divides and denominations – and the Pentecostals and the Evangelicals and the Anglicans, the Methodists, the Catholics, and all who revere My Name and the sacrifice of My Son shall unite with one heart and as one body. And that flame shall be seen across this land, and the cities and the villages of this nation shall start to burn with the fervency and the hunger of the Living God. For even as My Church has been bound by the shackles of compromise and passivity, I tell you that in this coming day and in this coming hour My firebrands shall start to rise.'

'And like Wilberforce, My apostolic voices shall rise in the Houses of Parliament. They shall arise in London; they shall arise in Edinburgh; they shall arise in the North of England and even as the unions had a voice in past years that was strident and rose above the crowds and became the voice of the masses – so in like manner shall My Church's voice start to be heard in a manner far above and beyond these present days.

And so I shall raise My apostles and they shall stand at the city gates and the gates of trading, and they shall stand in the government, and they shall stand in the media, and in the banking institutions and in businesses, and they shall stand in the clergy of this nation. And I shall raise up My prophets, and they shall rise, and their faces will be as flint, and even as John Knox' voice rang out above Scotland, I tell you that My prophet's voices shall start to rise in this nation. And I call My intercessors – I call My intercessors – Pray, Pray – do not desist from your prayers. For even that which you have perceived in your spirits and that which you have yearned for, it is almost upon you.

For surely the day of the missionaries dawns once more upon these shores. For surely the day of the Gospel going forth to the uttermost parts of the earth dawns once more upon these shores. And as My fire starts to fall across Great Britain, I tell you that the men, the women, boys and girls shall feel the call to leave theses isles and to travel to the continents of the earth to preach My Gospel. And a mighty flood of evangelists – a mighty throng of missionaries shall leave this nation – and I shall thrust them into the four corners of the earth. And they shall go to Japan, and they shall go to Beijing, and they shall go to Africa, East and West, and they shall go to Europe and to the Middle East. And I shall spread them as a net over the continent of Asia.

And I shall open doors to My Gospel that have previously been shut. Even the doors of iron and of brass shall be opened unto the missionaries from the British Isles – Vietnam, North Korea and beyond. And there shall be a great flood and a torrent of My Gospel that shall once more go forth from this land. And I shall send Bibles from this land, and I shall send resources – resources – resources from Great Britain – that will feed, that will clothe, that will build, that will teach, that will establish My Gospel in the four corners of the earth. For this is the destiny of this land in latter days,' says the Lord. "to resource, to nurture, to establish, to preach My Gospel. And even as in past days, this Empire was established, so I tell you that in this coming day and this coming hour it shall be the Empire of the Great King of Heaven that shall be established.

And there has yet to rise from these shores one who has a rod of iron – in the decades to come – you shall yet see one rise who has My government upon his shoulders – and he shall rise in the government, and he shall rise in this nation and he shall rule with a rod of iron,' says the Lord. 'And he will come at such a time when Great Britain is faltering – and I shall do this because of the prayers of My people. For there shall be a great swarm that shall rise against these isles in the decades to come. A great swarm as an army will arise across the waters around this nation, but this man with the rod of iron shall stand firm and the nation shall take courage, and the Lionheart of Britain shall arise as one, and the great swarm shall turn back and even in an instant be stopped in their tracks,' says the Lord.

'And there will be a great joining of the Lion and the Eagle. And even as the voices in the streets and the byways – the murmuring, the complaining of any alliance between the United States and Britain – so I tell you that these voices neither discern the times nor the purposes of the Living God. For even as the Eagle came to the Lion's aid in times gone by, so I tell you that in this coming season, once again this alliance between the Lion and the Eagle shall be forged and the forge shall not be broken,' says the Lord, 'because it is destined by Heaven. And a great wave of prayer shall rise up from the East Coast of America through the heartland to the West – and that wave of prayer and intercession shall wash across Britain as a fiercely burning flame and shall cleanse and protect. But in the years ahead, so the prayers of the saints in Britain shall rise and, like a wave, they shall spread across America and preserve and protect. And a great joining shall occur and this joining shall not be the joining of man,' says the Lord, 'but the joining of Almighty God. And this nation shall return to its Christian roots. It shall RETURN to its Christian roots – and the glory of the Lion of Judah shall once more return and rest upon the Lion. IF my people repent of the sins of this nation and humble themselves and pray.'"[17]

## Sources:

1. http://christianinternational.com/bishophamon/

2. https://richards-watch.org/prophecy-library-1909-2017/

3. http://www.prayforscotland.org.uk/smith-wigglesworths-1947-prophetic-word/

4. From the Lester Sumrall Facebook page Https://www.facebook.com/drlestersumrall/

5. https://www.calltothewall.org/tommy-hicks-vision-of-end-time-ministriesjuly-25-1961/

6. http://www.christianstogether.net/Articles/89889/Christians_Together_in/Christian_Life/Is_there_any/Jean_Darnalls_Vision.aspx

7. http://www.northwestprophetic.com/2009/07/two-winds-coming-to-church.html

8.http://www.byfaith.co.uk/prophecynow/prophecynow19.htm

9. https://richards-watch.org/prophecy-library-1909-2017/

10. http://ukpropheticwords.blogspot.co.uk/2013/02/the-uk-will-be-changed.html?q=kim+clement+2012

11. https://www.emic.org/blog/the-fourth-wave/

12.http://www.elijahlist.com/words/display_word.html?ID=16320

13. https://richards-watch.org/2016/01/16/revd-john-kilpatrick-prophecy-of-internet-harvest-of-souls/

14. https://richards-watch.org/tag/glory/page/2/

15.http://www.elijahlist.com/words/display_word.html?ID=13801

16. http://ukpropheticwords.blogspot.co.uk/2016/04/

17. Published by Cross Rhythms Christian music & media on 18 July 2005 and described as: A prophetic word for the UK given to Wendy Alec founder of GOD TV on 15/07/05.

# Chapter Six
# What Must We Do?

It is wonderful to read such inspiring prophetic calls to the fulness of God's glory and power in the world. To read of His power, His fire, His outpourings, is wonderful. But I want to leave you with a more down to earth response to all that God is doing in this new Church age.

> Probably the greatest thing we must realise, if we grasp the importance of the era in which we live, is that we must "live a life worthy of the calling we have received." (Ephesians 4:1)

You are incredibly important. Your decisions matter. Your church is important. You have been born "for such a time as this". I want to urge you to live with great significance.

My Great, great uncle was the explorer, pilot and sailor Sir Francis Chichester. He was renowned for his advances in navigation, his bold piloting of planes across the globe and subsequent sailing around the world, single handed.

At one point he travelled cross the Atlantic for many days before he realised the biscuit tin next to his compass was magnetic, which of course, adjusted his compass reading slightly.

He had been going off course for days!

Now, being slightly off course matters little for an hour, but days later he was miles from where he should have been.

I have found the same can be true in church life. As we go through the ups and downs, the challenges and joys of life, we can find a "magnetic biscuit tin" has lodged itself next to the compass of our hearts. It affects all our activities and, before long, we are more off course than we might ever know. Success, failure, power, conflict; these all come to buffet our hearts and if not tended to carefully, unseen powers can shift us off course.

> *Being off course one degree matters little on day one, but in year 10 or year 15, we are miles from the original plan of heaven for our churches, lives and lands.*

And what about a century or two later?

## The Sins of Jeroboam

Jeroboam followed King Solomon and brought idolatry to the high places of Israel, specifically in Dan and Bethel. This was wicked in God's sight. If you continue to read through 1 and 2 Kings, you'll discover that 15 generations later, the children of Israel were still, "continuing in the sins of Jeroboam". The ripple effects of his errors went unchecked.

What we do, how we choose to live, can echo for generations, unhindered. This is scary. We must make sure our echo is pure!

In my book *Stronger: Building a powerful interior world*, I told the story of Jonathan Edwards. An investigation into the famed 18th century revival preacher showed that, of the 1,394 known descendants of Jonathan Edwards, 100 became preachers and missionaries, 100 lawyers, 80 public officials, 75 army and navy officers, 65 college professors, 60 physicians, 60 prominent authors, 30 judges, 13 college presidents, 3 United States senators, and one a Vice-President of the United States. His generational echo was one of power, purity and divine influence.

Compare him with another man of that era, Max Jukes. Mr Jukes had 310 descendants who died as paupers, 150 were criminals, 100 were drunkards, 7 were murderers, and more than half of the women were prostitutes. His impurity and weakness also echoed for generations.

> It would seem that our decisions in life echo for a long time! You are going to leave behind a legacy of decisions, opinions and priorities. You must, in this vital Church Age, make sure your echo comes from our Fathers heart.

## The Ways of God

Like Moses, we need to ask God to "teach me your ways". Moses had stumbled across God in the form of a burning bush in the desert, but now he wanted to know how to access God's favour at will:

*"If you are pleased with me, teach me your ways so I may know you and continue to find favour with you."* (Exodus 33:13)

Moses wanted to continue to find God's favour, and he knew that if he knew God's ways, he could find God's favour.

God has WAYS that lead to favour. I don't know about you, but I don't want to just stumble across occasional favour, like Moses at the burning bush. I want to know how to walk in

God's blessing, goodness and favour every day, in every way! That would be an amazing life!

God's ways are like laws. By that I don't mean "rules," as in "commands", but more dynamic realities, like the law of gravity. There are ways in which God thinks; ways that He has made the world to work. If we cooperate with them, we will enjoy life in His favour.

You can disagree with the law of gravity all you want, but if you jump out of a plane, you will go down, not up! In just the same way, God has made the world to work in a certain way, spiritually and relationally. Discover those ways and you'll understand how God is intending to bless you and be able to cooperate with Him.

Ezekiel 47 talks of a river from God's temple. It swells to ankle, knee, then waist deep. Finally, it becomes *"a river you cannot cross"* (Ezekiel 47:5); a powerful movement that you cannot traverse. Your only choice is to go with it.

> The closer you get to God, the more you
> have to cooperate with His ways.

In the deep ends of God, where His glory is at work, He is untraversable, uncrossable. You must learn to cooperate with His methods in the coming season and not try to traverse them.

Now these ways are very simple, but they are not always easy. Like King David, let's pray Psalm 63:8:

"My soul follows hard AFTER you!"

I want to cling, cleave, stick with, follow closely and join myself to God and His ways, knowing that by doing that, I'll be blessed.

## The Ways of Jesus

As we face a new Church era, I want to leave you rooted in several simple ways of God. He has left us unchanging instructions that will not be adjusted by the changing seasons. These instructions worked through the early Church age, through the dark ages, the Reformation, and they will work until the end of the Church age.

They are simple, powerful, profound truths found in the Great Commission. But perhaps they will be presented here in ways you have never thought of. Let's first remind ourselves of His words:

> "Then Jesus came to them and said, 'All authority in heaven and on earth has been given to me. Therefore go and make disciples of all nations, baptising them in the name of the Father and of the Son and of the Holy Spirit, and teaching them to obey everything I have commanded you. And surely I am with you always, to the very end of the age.'" (Matthew 28:18-20)

> "He said to them, 'Go into all the world and preach the gospel to all creation. Whoever believes and is baptised will be saved, but whoever does not believe will be condemned. And these signs will accompany those who believe: In my name they will drive out demons; they will speak in new tongues; they will pick up snakes with their hands; and when they drink deadly poison, it will not hurt them at all; they will place their hands on sick people, and they will get well.'" (Mark 16:15-18)

## The Law of Baptism

The first unchanging truth the Great Commission teaches us,

and it is mentioned in both Matthew's and Mark's versions, is that the Kingdom comes by baptism Now I know this is speaking of baptism in water (in the main), but understand this in the broader sense. Christianity only really works when you are immersed in it.

> **What God is about to do will only work for the fully surrendered.**

There is nothing more miserable than a half-hearted Christian. Teetering on the edge of favour and glory, without the bottle to jump in and suck the juice out of God's "life in all it's fullness" is quite painful! The half-hearted usually end up aware of all the "do nots", but get to enjoy very few of the blessings.

In Christianity, you must be baptised. You probably already know that simply means, "immersed, dunked, saturated, marinated". Hobby Christianity will not work. Once every three weeks attenders will never know God's power! The Kingdom is for the immersed.

The Bible talks about being immersed (baptised) in water, into the Body of Christ (Church), in the Holy Spirit and even into suffering (Joy of joys! But there is no glory without suffering).

Baptism, or being immersed, speaks of letting go of an old life and fully embracing a new life. It is a burial of sorts and a coming back to life. It is accepting, "This is a revolution in my life. Everything's changed."

The Christian walk, and God's ways or laws, simply don't work by dipping your toe in. You either tithe or you don't. You worship or you don't. You obey or you don't. You can try to attend church occasionally instead of becoming a disciple (what God has called you to), but usually you are simply looking for enough of God to anaesthetise you from life's ills, or your own shame – but you'll never know His power to transform you. So you'll grow old, but not better. Wrinkled, but not mature! That's not a great destiny!

## Right Medicine, Wrong Dose

I remember spending months in Africa in the 1990s, most of it in malaria zones. I was on a course of malaria protection tablets that involved taking about 4 tablets a day, and I had been taking that dose for about 182 days. If I jumped up and down I rattled like a maraca!

One evening in the African bush I was popping my pills and a local friend (who was not taking malaria prevention) noticed me taking my dose. Having spotted a few mosquitos that day he paused and asked, "Can I have one please?"

I looked at my pills, then looked at him, wondering what to say. Taking these pills was the correct medicine, but taking a single pill was NOT the right dose. Right thing, wrong dose. A single malaria prevention tablet would do nothing.

> It's the same with the Gospel. This gospel is right, but the only dose that works is full immersion.

In this new era of divine purpose for the Church, we must make sure we are fully immersed in the purposes of God. The only way the Kingdom comes, is by full immersion in God's purposes.

Sometimes this can be counter-intuitive (as are many things in the Kingdom!) We think that living on the edges, dabbling, waiting to see what works, is the "sensible" way to follow God. Nothing could be further from the truth.

I recently read that the safest pilots in World War 2 were the most gung-ho ones. The more careful you tried to be, the more likely you were to be picked off and shot down! How counter intuitive is that?

## Mourning Comes Before Dancing

I grew up as a missionary kid in southern Europe, living in the sun, playing on boats, beaches and "off-roading" around Spain and Morocco. It was great. But when God called my parents, we didn't know it would be great. They had to immerse themselves (and us kids) in obedience BEFORE they knew it would be a blessing!

You see, my earliest memory of this part of my life, is not the fun of living abroad, but the shock of having to sell all my toys! My dad gave up his good job, my parents sold their house, we put everything we owned in a Citroen 2CV6 car and drove from Wales, homeless and jobless. All I really remember is my mother sobbing as we drove away from everything they'd tried to build up to that point. We had no idea it would go well – we were only aware of what we were losing. It was a death. An immersion. A baptism of suffering.

But that is where the Gospel becomes most powerful.

> When you TOTALLY surrender to God,
> He totally opens heaven's resources to you!

At the time you don't know it, but you just found one of the "ways" of God, and now you are going to continually find His favour.

There are loads of wonderful terms in the Bible for Christians: sons, heirs, children, sheep, soldiers, athletes.

But in Philemon 1:1, Paul uses this description to sum up his immersion in God's plan for his life:

*"I Paul, a prisoner of Jesus Christ..."*

He was actually a prisoner of Nero at the time of writing this, but he never saw it like that. He was a prisoner, a slave, a servant of God; in chains for the Gospel. Could you describe yourself in the same way? Could you say, "I'm locked into God's will, whatever and whereever that might be"?

When Jesus looked into the eyes of his "twelve" and said *"take up your cross and follow me,"* (Luke 9:23) it wasn't going to be a metaphorical cross. Most of them would indeed die for the truth they were discovering. Church history and tradition tells us Andrew died on a cross and so did Simon Peter, Phillip, Thaddeus and Simon the Zealot. Bartholomew was skinned alive. James son of Zebedee was beheaded; the other James beaten to death. Thomas was run through with a lance. Matthew was stabbed. All for this incredible Gospel they knew to be true, and for the love of their "older brother" Jesus.

> They immersed themselves in a new reality. Jesus was THE Way, the Truth and the Life, and they were going to live for Him, and even die for Him.

This world held little for them. They were now living for eternity.

I hope for you that obedience will not lead to martyrdom, and yet with a true eternal perspective, we would see that immense reward comes from our full baptism into God's will – even if it leads to the end of our life on earth.

Someone posted a photo and article on my Facebook page a while ago which showed the hanging of a Christian pastor.

A broad smile was stretched across his wonderful face right the way through the build-up, only drooping to a lifeless stare once he had died. There was more joy on that man's face as the noose was placed over his head than most faces in church on a Sunday morning.

It is amazing, isn't it, that while many around the world are dying for their faith, many of us won't live for Him.

> Martin Luther said, "A religion that gives nothing, costs nothing, and suffers nothing, is worth nothing."

What is the value of your religion?

Many like the idea of serving God and enjoying a fruitful destiny. As one writer put it, "Many wish to serve God, but in an advisory capacity only!"

What about you?

William Booth, founder of the Salvation Army, was going blind and his son was tasked with telling him the news that he would not see again. "Do you mean that I am going blind?" the General asked. "I hear we must contemplate that," his son replied.

"Son", said General Booth, "I have done what I could for God and for His people with my eyes. Now I shall do what I can for God without my eyes."

When we live in this utter immersion in God's will, it is true that there are days when it costs us everything, and our sobs of burial ring out as worship in heaven. But let me assure you, everyone that suffers will also know God's immense glory. His favour. His blessing in life.

This is one of the "Laws of Heaven".

## Make Disciples

The second great truth from the Great Commission is that we are to be, and make, disciples. This means that the Church should feel like a training school, a barracks, a college, a training camp.

But while Jesus said we should *make disciples*, we often think church is about running church services and projects. This, I believe, will become one of the great changes in the coming Church Age.

The Church was designed to become a powerful training centre sending millions of glory-carrying missionaries into every strata of society and into every corner of the earth.

> As we learn to train, instead of living to run good church services, we will be raising powerful people. The result will be that the church will run itself!

Until churches become training centres, we will find that people are often serving in the church for all sorts of reasons other than the one's God intended. The evidence of this is found in churches that abound with little "power bases", with people who will not invite or take feedback, and volunteers and staff who take way too much personal approval in life from the things they do.

Instead of serving Jesus many are looking for approval through works. Instead of service as an act of worship, some are deriving their worth from their roles. Instead of running after the goal of the Great Commission, we fall in love with our personal achievements.

One department in our church once said to me, "If you touch this area, we will leave the church." Of course, I HAD to touch that area then, because such ungodly, unchecked behaviour showed the utter lack of depth in a personal relationship with God!

It's as though some treat the act of service like Gollum from The Hobbit who loved the One Ring. They grasp areas of responsibility gurgling, "My precious", hugging power like some demonic ring of significance! People build castles around roles, old cultures, rotas, responsibilities. And what that screams is, "I am no longer growing. I want to settle here, and use this to give me significance. My intimacy with God has plateaued and I am now using the work to give me approval."

These power bases show that our churches lack disciples, sons and daughters. We've got everyone running Sunday services, projects and teams, but we've forgotten to raise disciples.

> You know whether you're raising sons or slaves, when you give someone feedback to improve their area of service.

"Do not rebuke mockers or they will hate you; rebuke the wise and they will love you," Proverbs 9:8 says. Every time I have encouraged a person to improve, grow, update, the sons rise to it, while the mockers turn it into a thing of confrontation and conflict.

In our own church, as I have given up trying to run great Sundays (as my main concern) and have instead built a training school at the heart of our church, I have found the dynamic power of the Kingdom has increased.

In all six sites of our multi-site church we have made it mandatory for all leaders to be in perpetual training, coaching and discipleship. I spend money on them. Give them books.

Take them on trips. Give time to grow then and support them.

The transformation has been incredible, especially in the area of lessening the ungodly powerbases. Instead I have a leadership of excited, appreciated, growing sons and daughters.

You see, my greatest resource, my gold, is not our buildings, my strategies or our technical equipment – it is the people! My leaders are my greatest gold, my loudest vision statements, my most powerful examples and my perfect billboards for values and vision! God does not rest upon organisations, but upon people.

And so I live to invest in them. To wash their feet. To make their lives the best they can possibly be.

I don't even want them to run church – I simply want to raise disciples, and trust that God will build His Church in the wake.

> Instead of growing a big church, I want to grow big people. It's more powerful, less ego-driven and definitely less stressful!

## Cabinet Re-Shuffles and Football Coaches

In discipleship cultures there are constant cabinet reshuffles, constant adjustments. Just like governments regularly shuffle the make-up of their leaders for maximum political effectiveness, we too should be adjusting for maximum power in a given season. To use another picture, it is as though I have become a football coach as a leader. My job is to train, support and constantly alter the team to the right roles at a given time.

The team that take a church from A to B, isn't usually the same team that takes it from B to C. Moving around, seasonal roles, some taking a rest, others taking more pressure – this is the world of the growing church. So you need disciples who love the team's goal, and are not just serving for their personal role. Flexibility is natural to disciples, but painful to power bases. Go after a flexible, discipleship culture with passion.

As we build churches of disciples, the feel of the church is going to change from an obsession with running great, attractional services (though that will happen), to raising an army of brave warriors.

> However you choose to do it – make church feel like a training college, a barracks, a school, and the powers of the Kingdom will begin to flood what you do!

## Go, Don't Settle!

The third great, unchanging truth from the Great Commission is that Jesus said, *"Go into all the world."*

Jesus said "Go." We often stay. We prefer to settle.

Perhaps it's fear driven, but it seems that most pastors and Christians obsess about accumulating, growing, gathering, when it seems Jesus tells us there is Kingdom power in going, sending and mission.

In Acts 1:8 Jesus said,

*"But you will receive power when the Holy Spirit comes on you; and you will be my witnesses in Jerusalem, and in all Judea and Samaria, and to the ends of the earth."*

Amazingly, the Spirit of God fell in Acts 2, but they stayed and enjoyed a Jewish revival for quite some time. In fact, in the end it was persecution that got them to rise up and go (Acts 8:1)!

## Dust Settles

Dust settles and we are made of dust. Our flesh is very good at settling, loving the familiar, accumulating power, people or wealth. But the Kingdom is a GO Kingdom! Something happens as we go.

The Church should feel like a movement, not a club. The moment it begins to feel like a club that exists to serve its members, divine power is leaking away. It IS better to give than receive. If we try to save our souls, we'll lose them. But if we lose our souls, we will gain them.

The church I lead is not particularly overflowing with evangelists. In fact, historically, we have been more of a worship and teaching centre, generally struggling to feel powerful in the area of evangelism.

But in response to a prophetic word from Jean Darnell, we planted three new locations in a single week. We took out 10 billboards, posted over 100,000 postcards through doors, pounded the streets in prayer and reached out with everything from hot dogs to healing. The result? 300 responded to Jesus! Since then we have moved out to six locations, and whenever we do, a fresh surge of power from heaven flows in our 100 year old church.

> **When we build in God's ways, we will receive God's power.**

Even the non-evangelist will find themselves having great conversations, leading people to Jesus, praying prayers they never imagined possible, if they will just find some way to go.

## The Paralysis of Over Analysis

I wonder if pastors sometimes get stuck in the *paralysis of over analysis,* waiting for the perfect moment to plant a new church or reach out:

"Perhaps we'll do that when the church reaches a certain size," they say. This can be a deception. You actually get stronger by going. The more you wait, the more you may just become weak and self-obsessed. Comfort will cloud the soul of your church. Safety will stall your engine. That's not where the Kingdom lives!

> *The Kingdom is counter-intuitive. The more you go, give, and live with a generous, pioneering heart, the more powerfully the Kingdom will come!*

Jesus, our perfect pioneer, showed us all about living as fearless pioneers. After just three and a half years of teaching His disciples He "retired", sat down at the right hand of the Father, and chose to empower His disciples from a distance! To many this would be WAY too soon! His disciples were far from mature and complete. But it was better that He went, as the power of God empowered the many to carry His Gospel of glory across the earth. (John 16:7)

In Church today we often find ourselves in roles for 20, 30, 40 years. We settle. We are no longer missional disciples and we are no longer going into all the world. We've plateaued and the power of the Kingdom no longer flows in our lives. Here's why I think that happens:

## The Enemies of GO

**1. Caution.** Often we feel weak, personally or corporately. But it is a deception to think strength will flow by becoming static, other than for short healing and development seasons. Leaders are often aware of a lack of staff, but Kingdom strength comes from a generous spirit, confidence in God and creating divine vacuums for God to fill. Sometimes, like Peter, we have to step out onto the waters of lack, to see Jesus come through with a miracle! Go plant that new church or reach a new nation – there's health and power in keeping your "Go" alive!

**2. Age.** Neurological studies have demonstrated a cognitive shift as we age, from right-brain creativity to left-brain memory. The danger? As we age, we stop leading out of imagination and start leading out of memory. When we are young we imagine the future and run towards it with passion. We can be anything – an astronaut, footballer, scientist. But as we age, we change biologically. If we are not careful, after a certain point we are no longer leading from imagination, but rather we are repeating what we have seen in the past. This leads us to repeating safe patterns of ministry, rather than striking out into new territory in God. Let God renew your youth like the eagles!

**3. Lack of Five-Fold Ministry.** Many churches who fail to recognise the reformation and restoration of the five-fold ministries in Ephesian 4 (apostles, prophets, evangelists, pastors, teachers) fall into maintenance mode and stop pioneering. Unless we have powerful pioneering apostolic, prophetic and evangelistic ministries investing into our churches we will plateau and settle, since pastors and teachers tend to most easily settle around whether people are happy and being taught the Bible.

This is not enough to change the world. Every church needs the evangelist to stir a passion for the lost, the prophet to be a catalyst towards the imminent power of God, and the apostle to coach us into God's masterplan to touch the globe. Make sure you are connected to apostles and prophets, or else the GO will depart from your church.

**4. Too Busy.** Because some churches lack a discipleship culture, they can often be hopeless at ending projects that aren't working, because no one can have truly honest conversations. The end result is that we are busy doing things that aren't working, and few people have the energy left to truly immerse themselves, be disciples, and embrace the mission to disciple the world. We must know how to stop old assignments, so that we have the time to do today's assignment.

**5. Tabernacle Syndrome.** I have spoken several times before in my books about Tabernacle Syndrome. In Luke 9 Peter, James and John are experiencing God's glory, and Peter says "Let's stay here." The Bible says he didn't know what he was saying, and Jesus marched them back down the mountain as there was divine work to do!

> Sometimes people of the Spirit want to stop in a place, a culture, a musical style or building when God moves.

It is as though they equate everything with that outpouring season as "holy." The result is that decades pass, they begin to look, feel and sound dated, and while the presence of God may be richly among them (as God's presence moves where there is hunger), they often tell me tearfully, "We have no young people left." The work usually dies out with the aging congregation. This common problem among Pentecostals requires a very bold, counter-intuitive, missional mindset, that even Peter lacked. A mindset that is determined to keep going to the lost, and adjusting our styles to be *"all things to all men"* (1 Corinthians 9:19-23), so that the world may be reached.

> The Church MUST retain her sense of movement and mission in these last days. Church should be gung-ho and pioneering, never settling in cosy communities and clubs.

The Church MUST be a training ground for world changers to be taught to carry God's glory. We must be disciples who are after the Kingdom goal of a world touched with glory, and not simply devote our lives to playing at church roles to feed our need for significance.

The only way to do this is to be baptised and immersed in God, His Spirit, His Word, His Will. We MUST be a generation utterly surrendered to the Father's love.

If we do these three, then the promise is that we will be a Church filled with glory.

## The Test of our Methods – The Kingdom Comes!

*"Whoever believes and is baptised will be saved, but whoever does not believe will be condemned. And these signs will accompany those who believe: In my name they will drive out demons; they will speak in new tongues; they will pick up snakes with their hands; and when they drink deadly poison, it will not hurt them at all; they will place their hands on sick people, and they will get well."* (Mark 16:15-18)

The result of churches and lives being built on the true north truths of Jesus' words in the Great Commission, is that the Kingdom will be seen among us.

Note that Jesus said signs would follow *those who believe* (not just the preachers). The community of believers will have authority over demonic realms, they'll speak in tongues, they will enjoy divine protection, and healings and miracles will abound.

This is a great test to see if we are building church right. In the book of Acts we read the following accounts of a church being built through immersion, discipleship and mission:

*"They devoted themselves to the apostles' teaching and to fellowship, to the breaking of bread and to prayer. Everyone was filled with awe at the many wonders and signs performed by the apostles. All the believers were together and had everything in common. They sold property and possessions to give to anyone who had need. Every day they continued to meet together in the temple courts. They broke bread in their homes and ate together with glad and sincere hearts, praising God and enjoying the favour of all the people. And the Lord added to their number daily those who were being saved."* (Acts 2:42-47)

*"All the believers were one in heart and mind. No one claimed that any of their possessions was their own, but they shared everything they had. With great power the apostles continued to testify to the resurrection of the Lord Jesus. And God's grace was so powerfully at work in them all that there were no needy persons among them. For from time to time those who owned land or houses sold them, brought the money from the*

*sales and put it at the apostles' feet, and it was distributed to anyone who had need."* (Acts 4:32-35)

*"The apostles performed many signs and wonders among the people. And all the believers used to meet together in Solomon's Colonnade. No one else dared join them, even though they were highly regarded by the people. Nevertheless, more and more men and women believed in the Lord and were added to their number. As a result, people brought the sick into the streets and laid them on beds and mats so that at least Peter's shadow might fall on some of them as he passed by. Crowds gathered also from the towns around Jerusalem, bringing their sick and those tormented by impure spirits, and all of them were healed."* (Acts 6:12-16)

In the coming Church Age it is not necessarily new or mystical theology that we'll need in order to transform society. Rather, we need to fully immerse in the Kingdom basics of discipleship, where ego is lost and the humility of passionate hunger for God leads us. And we must live for the "Go" of heaven, where a divine unction drives us in mission to every sphere of society and every nation of the earth.

> The result will be the glory of God sweeping the fully restored and reformed Church.

There will be power flowing through the fivefold ministries, and every other grace gift sent to us from Christ. Spiritual worship will build a throne for God's authority on earth, and the incredible presence of God will manifest richly among us.

This will result in a transformation of societies and nations that will sweep the world. Through God's glory upon us, we will literally begin to "disciple nations".

## The Church – The Home of Glory, Signs and Wonders

I love the apostle Paul's instructions about orderly worship in the book of first Corinthians. Even in his passion to create a bit of order in the immoral, yet spiritually gifted church, he says:

> *"But if an unbeliever or an inquirer comes in while everyone is prophesying, they are convicted of sin and are brought under judgment by all, as the secrets of their hearts are laid bare. So they will fall down and worship God, exclaiming, 'God is really among you!'"* (1 Corinthians 14:24-25)

> *Even in a tidy church setting, the apostle Paul believed unbelievers should be overcome by the presence and prophecy found in the church, to the point that they fall down under God's power.*

Our church broadcasts a weekly radio teaching programme across Europe. It is just 23 minutes of edited teaching time from our Sunday services and conferences. In all honesty, it's quite heavily edited to tidy it up.

One Sunday, some guests who had only ever heard us on the radio turned up to enjoy our service. As they entered the auditorium, they began to shake violently under the power of God's Spirit. I walked over to say hello, since they looked like visitors and were a little overcome by the atmosphere in the room.

Quickly explaining that they had only listened to our edited radio show, and shaking profoundly under God's power, they said "It's not like this on the radio is it?!"

It made me laugh so hard! Oh, I am so glad we don't have to edit out the power of God from our churches in real life! He should be mightily among us, powerfully present, gracious in glory and full of miracle manifestations!

## It's Real!

A dear friend took his young teenage son on a mission trip to Uganda, where God enabled this young 14-year old to see fifteen blind eyes open. His father recalled that his son sat, overwhelmed and shaking afterwards in his hotel room, amazed that God had used his prayers to see blind eyes open.

"It's real, Dad, it's real" he said.

It impacted this boy so deeply.

> Yes, God's presence should be real among us. We cannot, and should not, edit out the power of God from our churches.

These are the signs of God among us. If we fail to build a house that God loves, then what are we building?

I was once involved in leading a youth conference in worship. Not a lot had happened in the first few days, and it was day three and I had to lead worship. I was so intimidated about leading worship in an atmosphere where people hadn't really shown any hunger for God that I decided the only solution was for me to get so full, so drunk in the Spirit, so overwhelmed by God's presence, that I wouldn't really care what happened!

In the prayer meeting before the service I became overwhelmed by the presence of God and fell to the floor. I was so drunk in the Spirit that I couldn't stand up, and the band had to start the service without me. Eventually I crawled onto the platform, in an absolutely spiritually inebriated state, and stood looking at the 1,000 youth that had all been essentially, quite bored … until now.

The atmosphere changed. They could see something was happening in me. They could tell this wasn't going to be a normal meeting. We weren't going to play church any more. We weren't going to just sing another three fast songs, three slow songs, then have someone preach. I had been touched by heaven and an overflow was about to take place.

I whispered to the gathered youth, "Raise your hands and receive the Holy Spirit."

Slowly, one by one, young people began to fall under the power of the Holy Spirit around the auditorium. For three hours we sang one song, lost in worship. Many fell to the floor; some ran out to a cafeteria next door where an evangelist friend delivered them from their demonic issues! It was divine chaos!

The glory of God had visited that little conference. It was a few hours of heaven on earth.

But I believe we are coming to a season when the glory of God is going to reside as never before. The result of a Church fully immersed, fully discipled and fully committed to the GO of the Commission, is that we will be filled with glory, signs and wonders.

God will call us "Home". He will walk among us and…

*"The earth will be filled with the knowledge of the glory of the Lord, as the waters over the sea."* (Habakkuk 2:14)

# Epilogue

*"After two days He will revive us; on the third day He will restore us, that we may live in His presence. Let us acknowledge the LORD; let us press on to acknowledge Him. As surely as the sun rises, He will appear; He will come to us like the winter rains, like the spring rains that water the earth."* (Hosea 6:1-6)

I love these verses. They teach us how to change the spiritual climate. They say that we if acknowledge God (literally "press on to experience Him"), then He will pour out upon us like rain. When it rains, the desert becomes fruitful, agriculture flourishes and the thirsty drink. We need God to rain on our lives, our churches, our nations if we are to know an Age of Glory. Let me show what it means to "press on to experience Him":

In 1990 I was a worship leader of a small Bible school. In all honesty, I was struggling with my prayer life, but one Thursday evening as I led worship, the presence of God flooded the room with glory. We all sang in tongues without the need for a structured song for some time. It was as though God walked into the sanctuary.

As I sat at the piano, playing, my heart overwhelmed by His presence, I began to ask God, *What should I do?*

"Come away, come away," was the whispered reply.

Straight after that meeting I asked the college administrator if I could use a prayer apartment that the Bible College owned in another village. Amazingly, it was free that very weekend.

I remember it like it was yesterday. It was November 1990 in the village of Shere, West Sussex. I let myself into the small, cold apartment. Turning on everything that could possibly create a little heat (the oven, candles, the old three-bar fire!), I knelt in the living room to seek God's face, accompanied by my Bible, some paper and a pen.

As I knelt, God walked back into the room. For eight hours I cried, I wrote, I listened as God spoke to me about my life, His plans, things I needed to change, things He intended to do. I was overwhelmed, undone, electrified, humbled.

I returned to the Bible school the next day wondering what would happen next. As I went into my bedroom at the college and closed the door, God walked into the room *again*. I fell to my knees, reached for my pad and pen and began to write as God spoke to me. For four months, several hours a day, God would walk into my room and speak to me, overwhelming me, instructing me, lifting me to a new dimension.

It was in this time that I first experienced the climate change of heaven. God began to speak to me, His voice so clear. It seemed easier to pray than to *not* pray. Suddenly there was authority in the things I did and the prayers I prayed. We would go on mission, see incredible miracles, and return with joy, overwhelmed by the power of the Holy Spirit as waves of God's presence swept through everything we did for several months.

## Press on to Experience Him

It began to "rain" because I had given time to "press on to experience Him". Perhaps the simplest, yet most profound response to this little prophetic book is to urge us all to "Seek God!" and press in for a deeper experience of Him than ever before.

Let's not get taken up with the distractions and the dullness of everyday life. Instead, let's start to think about how we can begin to seek God more. Is it moments in the morning, space across lunchtime, staying up later in the evening to seek His face? Is it taking a day off work, or giving up the occasional Saturday? Is it booking into a conference somewhere to go and find him afresh? Whenever I go to a conference I love the individual sessions, but really it's all the other spaces around it where I can focus on seeking God that seem most productive. Resting, listening, away from my routine is so powerful.

Leaders, will your church set aside nights to pray occasionally? Could you shut down every project for several weeks at certain times of the year and give that same time to seek God as a church? Will you send some of your key leaders to places that will stir afresh their intimate longing for God? It will be worth the spend! Send them! Encourage your leaders, your young people, your busy businessmen, to seek God.

When a culture of seeking God fills our churches it changes the climate. It begins to rain; fruit comes more easily, everything flourishes, everything grows. Authority is heightened. Prophecy is clearer. Miracles are easier. Salvations are more frequent. Peace is more prevalent. Healing is quicker. Comfort is felt. Even the sense of God's presence in our services is richer, causing the unsaved to tremble in God's presence, and fall overwhelmed by God's power and get up saved!

And if we seek Him, then we will align our lives and churches for the coming Church Age. We will become sensitive to the voice of heaven. Aligned closely to the instructions of the Shepherd of our souls, perhaps we will hear the Darling of Heaven sing:

*"Arise, shine, for your light has come,*
*and my glory rises upon you.*
*See, darkness covers the earth*
*and thick darkness is over the peoples,*
*but I AM arising upon you*
*and my glory is appearing over you*
*Nations will come to your light,*
*and kings to the brightness of your dawn.*
*Lift up your eyes and look about you:*
*All assemble and come to you;*
*your sons come from afar,*
*and your daughters are carried on the hip.*
*Then you will look and be radiant,*
*your heart will throb and swell with joy;*
*the wealth on the seas will be brought to you,*
*to you the riches of the nations will come...*
*...and I will adorn YOU, my glorious temple with GLORY."*

(Based on Isaiah 60:1-7)

# About the Author

Jarrod Cooper is an inspirer. Using teaching, song and prophetic ministry he aims to inspire the Church to fullness in Jesus.

He leads Revive Church, a multi-site church meeting across Hull and East Yorkshire in the United Kingdom. He is an author, songwriter, conference speaker and broadcaster. His 30 minute radio shows, REVIVE and Days of Wonder air in several dozen nations.

Revive Church is devoted to inspiring revival, aiming to build and plant great God-filled churches and campuses. They also conduct revival events where God's glory moves, people are saved, leaders inspired and miracles abound!

Jarrod is married to Victoria, is dad to Zach, and loves travelling, skiing, food, great coffee and the presence of God! Together they run Deep Blue Publishing which releases songs, albums, books and online courses and Revive Academy, their leadership and arts training school.

# Books by Jarrod Cooper

*Believe and Confess (with Victoria Cooper)*

*Stronger: Building a powerful interior world*

*When Spirit & Word Collide*

*Glory in the Church*

# Online Courses by Jarrod Cooper

*Moving in Healing, Miracles & Prophecy*

*Stronger: Building a powerful interior world*

*When Spirit & Word Collide: Prophetic Leadership in the 21st century*

**Download a free worship album by Jarrod from:**
**www.JarrodCooper.net**

Printed in Poland
by Amazon Fulfillment
Poland Sp. z o.o., Wrocław